March of America Facsimile Series

Number 45

Expedition Against the Ohio Indians

William Smith

Expedition Against the Ohio Indians

by William Smith

ANN ARBOR

UNIVERSITY MICROFILMS, INC.

A Subsidiary of Xerox Corporation

Foreword

General Braddock's defeat by a numerically inferior French and Indian force near Fort Duquesne in 1775 was a classic example of the ineffectiveness of European military tactics when employed in the North American wilderness. *An Historical Account of the Expedition against the Ohio Indians, in the Year 1764. Under the Command of Henry Bouquet* explains how one British commander profited from that bitter lesson and successfully adapted his tactics to the frontier. The book, which is believed to have been written by Dr. William Smith, Provost of the College of Philadelphia, was published in 1765. By his own admission Smith was greatly aided in the composition of his book by papers which an officer of long experience made available to him. The officer, unidentified by the author, had drafted the papers for his own edification, "but being told that they might convey many useful hints to others, and be of much service if laid before the public...was pleased upon my request, freely to communicate them to me for that purpose." Smith wished to show how battles ought to be fought in the wilderness and he tried to prove his point by using the example of Colonel Bouquet.

Henry Bouquet, of Swiss origin, belonged to that class of professional soldiers which flourished in the 18th century. He had served in the armies of several countries before entering the English army. Sent to North America during the period of the French and Indian War, he fought in a number of engagements. Although the war terminated in 1763 with England the victor, the frontier areas of the North American colonies continued to be troubled by Indian attacks. One of the principal reasons for the unrest was ascribed by the author to "a jealousy of our growing power... They probably imagined that they beheld in 'every little garrison the germ of a future colony.'" One of the most exposed strongpoints held by the English was Fort Pitt. Consequently Colonel Bouquet was ordered in 1763 to bring supplies and reinforcements to the garrison. As Bouquet and the men of the relief column neared the Fort, the "fate of Braddock was every moment before their eyes." But when the Indian attack came, Bouquet was ready. Electing to fight the Indians on their own terms, Colonel Bouquet defeated them roundly at Bushy Run. The relief column reached Fort Pitt several days later and forced the Indians to lift their siege.

The next year, Colonel Bouquet followed up his success at Bushy Run by proceeding deep into Indian territory to pacify the "Ohio Indians." His reputation, won at Bushy Run, had preceded him. When the Indians saw him approaching with a force of approximately 1,500 men, they preferred peace to war. Thanks to Colonel Bouquet's display of power, commented the author, "we now have the pleasure once more to behold the temple of Janus shut, in this western world!"

Appended to the narrative of Bouquet's expeditions is a section entitled "Reflections on the War with the Savages of North-America." Here, in more systematic fashion, the author analyzed the character of the Indians, their mode of life, and their manner of fighting. He explained in considerable detail how England and the colonies ought to organize and to equip armies against them, and how forts ought to be constructed to repel their attacks.

The author included several battle plans and appendix material useful for combat against the Indians. Francis Parkman has supplied additional background for the book in *Historical Account of Bouquet's Expedition Against the Ohio Indians in 1764* (Cincinnati, 1868), pp. xi-xvi. Also useful is the article of J. C. Reeve, "Henry Bouquet, His Indian Campaigns," *Ohio Archaeological and Historical Quarterly*, XXVI (October, 1917), pp. 489-505.

Expedition Against the Ohio Indians

A N
HISTORICAL ACCOUNT

OF THE
EXPEDITION
AGAINST THE
OHIO INDIANS, in the YEAR 1764,

UNDER THE COMMAND OF
HENRY BOUQUET, Esq:

COLONEL of Foot, and now BRIGADIER GENERAL in AMERICA.

INCLUDING

His Transactions with the Indians, relative to the delivery of their prisoners, and the preliminaries of PEACE.

WITH AN
INTRODUCTORY ACCOUNT

Of the Preceeding Campaign, and Battle at BUSHY-RUN.

TO WHICH ARE ANNEXED
MILITARY PAPERS,

CONTAINING

Reflections on the war with the Savages; a method of forming frontier settlements; some account of the Indian country, with a list of nations, fighting men, towns, distances and different routs.

The whole illustrated with a Map and Copper-plates.

Published from authentic Documents, by a Lover of his Country.

PHILADELPHIA:

PRINTED and sold by WILLIAM BRADFORD, at the LONDON COFFEE-HOUSE, the corner of Market and Front-streets. M.DCC.LXV.

Neque multum Albici noſtris virtute cedebant, homines aſperi, et monta-
ni, exercitati in armis.   Cæs. Com. Bell. civ.

Plebs ruſtica, quæ ſub dio nutritur, ſolis patiens, deliciarum ignara,
ſimplicis animi, parvo contenta, duratis ad omnem laborum tolerantiam
membris----   Vegetius.

INTRODUCTION.

T H E general peace, concluded between Great-Britain, France and Spain, in the year 1762, altho' viewed in different lights by persons variously affected in the mother country, was nevertheless universally considered as a most happy event in America.

To behold the French, who had so long instigated and supported the Indians, in the most destructive wars and cruel depredations on our frontier settlements, at last compelled to cede all Canada, and restricted to the western side of Mississippi, was what we had long wished, but scarcely hoped an accomplishment of in our own days. The precision with which our boundaries were expressed, admitted of no ground for future disputes, and was matter of exultation to every one who understood and regarded the interest of these colonies. We had now the pleasing prospect of " entire * security from all " molestation of the Indians, since French intrigues could no longer be em- " ployed to seduce, or French force to support, them."

" UNHAPPILY, however, we were disappointed in this expectation. Our " danger arose from that very quarter, in which we imagined ourselves " in the most perfect security; and just at the time when we concluded the " Indians to be entirely awed, and almost subjected by our power, they sud- " denly fell upon the frontiers of our most valuable settlements, and upon all " our out-lying forts, with such unanimity in the design, and with such sa- " vage fury in the attack, as we had not experienced, even in the hottest " times of any former war."

A 2   SEVERAL

* The several quotations in this introduction are taken from the Annual Register, 1763, which is written with great elegance and truth, so far as the author appears to have been furnished with materials.

SEVERAL reasons have been assigned for this perfidious conduct on their part; such as an omission of the usual presents, and some settlements made on lands not yet purchased from them. But these causes, if true, could only affect a few tribes, and never could have formed so general a combination against us. The true reason seems to have been a jealousy of our growing power, heightened by their seeing the French almost wholly driven out of America, and a number of forts now possessed by us, which commanded the great lakes and rivers communicating with them, and awed the whole Indian country. They probably imagined that they beheld " in every little garrison the germ of a fu- " ture colony," and thought it incumbent on them to make one general and timely effort to crush our power in the birth.

By the papers in the Appendix, a general idea may be formed of the strength of the different Indian nations surrounding our settlements, and their situation with respect to each other.

THE Shawanese, Delawares and other Ohio tribes, took the lead in this war, and seem to have begun it rather too precipitately, before the other tribes in confederacy with them, were ready for action.

THEIR scheme appears to have been projected with much deliberate mischief in the intention, and more than usual skill in the system of execution. They were to make one general and sudden attack upon our frontier settlements in the time of harvest, to destroy our men, corn, cattle, &c. as far as they could penetrate, and to starve our out-posts, by cutting off their supplies, and all communication with the inhabitants of the Provinces.

IN pursuance of this bold and bloody project, they fell suddenly upon our traders whom they had invited into their country, murdered many of them, and made one general plunder of their effects, to an immense value.

THE frontiers of Pennsylvania, Maryland and Virginia, were immediately over-run with scalping parties, marking their way with blood and devastation

wherever

wherever they came, and all those examples of savage cruelty, which never fail to accompany an Indian war.

ALL our out-forts, even at the remotest distances, were attacked about the same time; and the following ones soon fell into the enemies hands---- viz. Le Boeuf, Venango, and Presqu' Isle, on and near lake Erie; La Bay upon lake Michigan; St. Joseph's, upon the river of that Name; Miamis upon the Miamis river; Ouachtanon upon the Ouabache; Sandusky upon lake Junundat; and Michilimackinac.

BEING but weakly garrisoned, trusting to the security of a general peace so lately established, unable to obtain the least intelligence from the colonies, or from each other, and being separately persuaded by their treacherous and savage assailants that they had carried every other place before them, it could not be expected that these small posts could hold out long; and the fate of their garrisons is terrible to relate.

THE news of their surrender, and the continued ravages of the enemy, struck all America with consternation, and depopulated a great part of our frontiers. We now saw most of those posts, suddenly wrested from us, which had been the great object of the late war, and one of the principal advantages acquired by the peace. Only the forts of Niagara, the Detroit and Fort-Pitt, remained in our hands, of all that had been purchased with so much blood and treasure. But these were places of consequence, and we hope it will ever remain an argument of their importance, and of the attention that should be paid to their future support, that they alone continued to awe the whole power of the Indians, and balanc'd the fate of the war between them and us!

THESE forts, being larger, were better garrisoned and supplied to stand a siege of some length, than the places that fell. Niagara was not attacked, the enemy judging it too strong.

THE officers who commanded the other two deserved the highest honor for the firmness with which they defended them, and the hardships they sustained rather than deliver up places of such importance,

MAJOR

MAJOR GLADWIN in particular, who commanded at the Detroit, had to withstand the united and vigorous attacks of all the nations living upon the Lakes.

THE design of this publication, and the materials in my hands, lead me more immediately to speak of the defence and relief of Fort Pitt.

THE Indians had early surrounded that place, and cut off all communication from it, even by message. Tho' they had no cannon, nor understood the methods of a regular siege, yet, with incredible boldness, they posted themselves under the banks of both rivers ‡ by the walls of the fort, and continued as it were buried there, from day to day, with astonishing patience; pouring in an incessant storm of musquetry and fire arrows; hoping at length, by famine, by fire, or by harrassing out the garrison, to carry their point.

CAPT. ECUYER, who commanded there, tho' he wanted several necessaries for sustaining a siege, and the fortifications had been greatly damaged by the floods, took all the precautions which art and judgement could suggest for the repair of the place, and repulsing the enemy. His garrison, joined by the inhabitants, and surviving traders who had taken refuge there, seconded his efforts with resolution. Their situation was alarming, being remote from all immediate assistance, and having to deal with an enemy from whom they had no mercy to expect.

GENERAL AMHERST, the commander in chief, not being able to provide in time for the safety of the remote posts, bent his chief attention to the relief of the Detroit, Niagara, and Fort-Pitt. The communication with the two former was chiefly by water, from the province of New-York; and it was on that account the more easy to throw succours into them. The detachment sent to the Detroit arrived there on the 29th of July, 1763; but Capt. Dalyell who commanded that detachment, and seventy of his men, lost their lives in a rencounter with the Indians near the fort. Previous to this disaster he had passed thro' Niagara, and left a reinforcement there.

FORT

‡ The Ohio and Monongahela, at the junction of which stands Fort Pitt.

FORT-PITT remained all this while in a moft critical fituation. No account could be obtained from the garrifon, nor any relief fent to it, but by a long and tedious land march of near 200 miles beyond the fettlements; and through thofe dangerous paffes where the fate of Braddock and others ftill rifes on the imagination.

COL. BOUQUET was appointed to march to the relief of this fort, with a large quantity of military ftores and provifions, efcorted by the fhattered re-mainder of the 42d and 77th regiments, lately returned in a difmal condition from the Weft-Indies, and far from being recovered of their fatigues at the fiege of the Havannah. General Amherft, having at that time no other troops to fpare, was obliged to employ them in a fervice which would have required men of the ftrongeft conftitution and vigour.

EARLY orders had been given to prepare a convoy of provifions on the fron-tiers of Pennfylvania, but fuch were the univerfal terror and confternation of the inhabitants, that when Col. BOUQUET arrived at Carlifle, nothing had yet been done. A great number of the plantations had been plundered and burnt, by the favages; many of the mills deftroyed, and the full-ripe crops ftood waving in the field, ready for the fickle, but the reapers were not to be found !

THE greateft part of the county of Cumberland, thro' which the army had to pafs, was deferted, and the roads were covered with diftreffed families, flying from their fettlements, and deftitute of all the neceffaries of life.

IN the midft of that general confufion, the fupplies neceffary for the expe-dition became very precarious, nor was it lefs difficult to procure horfes and carriages for the ufe of the troops.

THE commander found that, inftead of expecting fuch fupplies from a mife-rable people, he himfelf was called by the voice of humanity to beftow on them

fome

share of his own provisions to relieve their present exigency. However, in 18 days after his arrival at Carlisle, by the prudent and active measures which he pursued, joined to his knowlege of the country, and the diligence of the persons he employed, the convoy and carriages were procured with the assistance of the interior parts of the country, and the army proceeded.

THEIR march did not abate the fears of the dejected inhabitants. They knew the strength and ferocity of the enemy. They remembered the former defeats even of our best troops, and were full of diffidence and apprehensions on beholding the small number and sickly state of the regulars employed in this expedition. Without the least hopes, therefore, of success, they seemed only to wait for the fatal event, which they dreaded, to abandon all the country beyond the Susquehannah.

IN such despondency of mind, it is not surprising, that tho' their whole was at stake, and depended intirely upon the fate of this little army, none of them offered to assist in the defence of the country, by joining the expedition; in which they would have been of infinite service, being in general well acquainted with the woods, and excellent markmen.

IT cannot be contested that the defeat of the regular troops on this occasion, would have left the province of Pennsylvania in paticular, exposed to the most imminent danger, from a victorious, daring, and barbarous enemy; for (excepting the frontier people of Cumberland county) the bulk of its industrious inhabitants is composed of merchants, tradesmen and farmers, unaccustomed to arms, and without a militia law.

THE legislature ordered, indeed, 700 men to be raised for the protection of the frontiers during the harvest; but what dependence could be placed in raw troops, newly raised and undisciplined? Under so many discouraging circumstances, the Colonel (deprived of all assistance from the provinces, and having none to expect from the General, who had sent him the last man that could be removed from the hospitals) had nothing else to trust to, but about

500

500 soldiers of approved courage and refolution indeed, but infirm and intire strangers to the woods, and to this new kind of war. A number of them were even fo weak, as not to be able to march, and fixty were carried in waggons to reinforce the garrifons of the fmall pofts on the communication.

MEANWHILE Fort-Ligonier, fituated beyond the Allegheny-Mountains, was in the greateft danger of falling into the hands of the enemy, before the army could reach it. The ftockade being very bad, and the garrifon extremely weak, they had attacked it vigoroufly but had been repulfed by the bravery and good conduct of Lieutenant Blane who commanded there.

THE prefervation of that poft was of the utmoft confequence, on account of its fituation and the quantity of military ftores it contained, which if the enemy could have got poffeffion of, would have enabled them to continue their attack upon Fort-Pitt, and reduced the army to the greateft ftreights. For an object of that importance, every rifk was to be run ; and the Colonel determined to fend through the woods, with proper guides, a party of thirty men to join that garrifon. They fucceeded by forced marches in that hazardous attempt, not having been difcovered by the enemy till they came within fight of the Fort, into which they threw themfelves, after receiving fome running fhot.

THIS poft being fecured, the Colonel advanced to the remoteft verge of our fettlements, where he could receive no fort of intelligence of the number, pofition, or motions of the enemy. " This is often a very embarraffing cir-
" cumftance in the conduct of a campaign in America. The Indians had better
" intelligence, and no fooner were they informed of the march of our Army,
" than they broke up the fiege of Fort-Pitt, and took the rout by which they
" knew we were to proceed, refolved to take the firft advantageous opportu-
" nity of an attack on the march. "

IN this uncertainty of intelligence under which the Colonel laboured, as foon as he reach'd Fort-Ligonier, he determined very prudently to leave his waggons at that poft, and to proceed only with the pack horfes. Thus dif-

b   burdened

burdened, the army continued their rout. Before them lay a dangerous defile at Turtle Creek, several miles in length, commanded the whole way by high and craggy hills. This defile he intended to have passed the ensuing night, by a double or forced march; thereby, if possible, to elude the vigilance of so alert an enemy, proposing only to make a short halt in his way, to refresh the Troops, at Bushy-run.

WHEN they came within half a mile of that place, about one in the afternoon, (August 5th 1763) after an harrassing march of seventeen miles, and just as they were expecting to relax from their fatigue, they were suddenly attacked by the Indians, on their advanced guard; which being speedily and firmly supported, the enemy was beat off, and even pursued to a considerable distance.

' BUT * the flight of these barbarians must often be considered as a part of
' the engagement, (if we may use the expression) rather than a dereliction of
' the field. The moment the pursuit ended, they returned with renewed
' vigour to the attack. Several other parties, who had been in ambush in
' some high grounds which lay along the flanks of the army, now started up
' at once, and falling with a resolution equal to that of their companions,
' galled our troops with a most obstinate fire.

' IT was necessary to make a general charge with the whole line to dislodge
' them from these heights. This charge succeeded; but still the success
' produced no decisive advantage; for as soon as the savages were driven
' from one post, they still appeared on another, till by constant rein-
' forcements they were at length able to surround the whole detachment, and
' attack the convoy which had been left in the rear.

'THIS Manœuvre obliged the main body to fall back in order to protect it.
' The action, which grew every moment hotter and hotter, now became
' general. Our troops were attacked on every side; the savages supported
                                                                    ' their

* The above quotation is from the writer already mentioned, and seems so accurately and elegantly drawn up, from the account of this engagement, sent to his Majesty's ministers, that nothing better can be inserted in its room. There are but one or two small mistakes in it, which are here corrected.

' their fpirit throughout; but the fteady behaviour of the Englifh troops,
' who were not thrown into the leaft confufion by the very difcouraging
' nature of this fervice, in the end prevailed; they repulfed the enemy, and
' drove them from all their pofts with fixed bayonets.

' THE engagement ended only with the day, having continued from one
' without any intermiffion.

THE ground, on which the action ended, was not altogether inconvenient
' for an encampment. The convoy and the wounded were in the middle, and
' the troops, difpofed in a circle, incompaffed the whole. In this manner, and
' with little repofe, they paffed an anxious night, obliged to the ftricteft vi-
' gilance by an enterprizing enemy who had furrounded them.

' THOSE who have only experienced the feverities and dangers of a cam-
' paign in Europe, can fcarcely form an idea of what is to be done and en-
' dured in an American war. To act in a country cultivated and inhabited,
' where roads are made, magazines are eftablifhed, and hofpitals provided;
' where there are good towns to retreat to in cafe of misfortune; or, at the
' worft, a generous enemy to yield to, from whom no confolation, but the
' honour of victory, can be wanting; this may be confidered as the exercife
' of a fpirited and adventurous mind, rather than a rigid conteft where all is
' at ftake, and mutual deftruction the object : and as a contention between
' rivals for glory, rather than a real ftruggle between fanguinary enemies.
' But in an American campaign every thing is terrible; the face of the coun-
' try, the climate, the enemy. There is no refrefhment for the healthy, nor
' relief for the fick. A vaft unhofpitable defart, unfafe and treacherous, fur-
' rounds them, where victories are not decifive, but defeats are ruinous; and
' fimple death is the leaft misfortune, which can happen to them. This
' forms a fervice truely critical, in which all the firmnefs of the body and
' mind is put to the fevereft trial; and all the exertions of courage and addrefs
' are called out. If the actions of thefe rude campaigns are of lefs dignity,
' the adventures in them are more interefting to the heart, and more amufing
' to the imagination, than the events of a regular war.

BUT

INTRODUCTION

' But to return to the party of English, whom we left in the woods. At
' the first dawn of light the savages began to declare themselves, all about
' the camp, at the distance of about 500 yards; and by shouting and yelling
' in the most horrid manner, quite round that extensive circumference, en-
' deavoured to strike terror by an ostentation of their numbers, and their
' ferocity.

' After this alarming preparative, they attacked our forces, and, under
' the favour of an incessant fire, made several bold efforts to penetrate into
' the camp. They were repulsed in every attempt, but by no means dis-
' couraged from new ones. Our troops, continually victorious, were continually
' in danger. They were besides extremely fatigued with a long march, and
' with the equally long action, of the preceding day; and they were distressed
' to the last degree by a total want of water, much more intolerable than the
' enemy's fire.

' Tied to their convoy, they could not lose sight of it for a moment, with-
' out exposing, not only that interesting object, but their wounded men, to
' fall a prey to the savages, who pressed them on every side. To move was
' impracticable. Many of the horses were lost, and many of the drivers,
' stupefied by their fears, hid themselves in the bushes, and were incapable
' of hearing or obeying orders.

' Their situation became extremely critical and perplexing, having experi-
' enced that the most lively efforts made no impression upon an enemy, who
' always gave way when pressed; but who, the moment the pursuit was over
' returned with as much alacrity as ever to the attack. Besieged rather than
' engaged; attacked without interruption, and without decision; able neither
' to advance nor to retreat, they saw before them the most melancholy pros-
' pect of crumbling away by degrees, and entirely perishing without revenge
' or honor, in the midst of those dreadful desarts. The fate of Brad-
' dock was every moment before their eyes; but they were more ably con-
' ducted.

THE

' THE commander was fenfible that every thing depended upon bringing
' the favages to a clofe engagement, and to ftand their ground when attack-
' ed. Their audacioufnefs, which had increafed with their fuccefs, feemed
' favourable to this defign. He endeavoured, therefore, to increafe their con-
' fidence as much as poffible.

' FOR that purpofe he contrived the following ftratagem. Our troops
' were pofted on an eminence, and formed a circle round their convoy from
' the preceding night, which order they ftill retained. Col. BOUQUET gave
' directions, that two companies of his troops, who had been pofted in the
' moft advanced fituations, fhould fall within the circle; the troops on the
' right and left immediately opened their files, and filled up the vacant fpace,
' that they might feem to cover their retreat. Another company of light in-
' fantry, with one of grenadiers, were ordered " to lie in ambufcade," to
' fupport the two firft companies of grenadiers, who moved on the feigned
' retreat, and were intended to begin the real attack. The difpofitions were
' well made, and the plan executed without the leaft confufion.

' THE favages gave entirely into the fnare. The thin line of troops, which
' took poffeffion of the gound which the two companies of light foot had left,
' being brought in nearer to the center of the circle, the barbarians miftook
' thofe motions for a retreat, abandoned the woods which covered them, hur-
' ried headlong on, and advancing with the moft daring intrepidity, galled
' the Englifh troops with their heavy fire. But at the very moment when,
' certain of fuecefs, they thought themfelves mafters of the camp, the two
' firft companies made a fudden turn, and fallying out from a part of the hill,
' which could not be obferved, fell furioufly upon their right flank.

' THE favages, though they found themfelves difappointed and expofed,
' preferved their recollection, and refolutely returned the fire which they
' had received. Then it was the fuperiority of combined ftrength and dif-
' cipline appeared. On the fecond charge they could no longer fuftain the
' irrefiftible fhock of the regular troops, who rufhing upon them, killed
' many and put the reft to flight.

AT

' At the inftant when the favages betook themfelves to flight, the other
' two companies, which had been ordered to fupport the firft, rofe " from
" the ambufcade," marched to the enemy, and gave them their full fire. This
' accomplifhed their defeat. The four companies now united, did not give
' them time to look behind them, but purfued the enemy till they were
' totally difperfed.

' The other bodies of the favages attempted nothing. They were kept
' in awe during the engagement by the reft of the Britifh toops, who were
' fo pofted as to be ready to fall on them upon the leaft motion. Having
' been witneffes to the defeat of their companions, without any effort to fup-
' port or affift them, they at length followed their example and fled.

' This judicious and fuccefsful manœuvre refcued the party from the
' moft imminent danger. The victory fecured the field, and cleared all the
' adjacent woods. But ftill the march was fo difficult, and the army had fuf-
' fered fo much and fo many horfes were loft, that before they were able
' to proceed ' they were reluctantly o bliged to deftroy fuch part of their
convoy of provifions as they could not carry with them for want of horfes.
Being lightened by this facrifice, they proceeded to Bufhy-Run, where
finding water, they encamped.

A plan of this engagement is annexed, and it was thought the more neceffary here to infert a particular account of it, as the new * manœuvres and
fkilful conduct of the commander, feem to have been the principal means,
not only of preferving his army in the moft critical fituation, but likwife of
enfuring them a compleat victory.

The enemy loft about fixty men on this occafion, fome of them their chief
warriors ; which they reputed a very fevere ftroke. They had likewife many
wounded in the purfuit. The Englifh loft about fifty men and had about fixty
wounded.   The

* Another reafon for being fo particular in this account, is that the military papers annexed to
this work, and the plan for carrying on any future war with the Indians, were compofed upon the
experience of this engagement, by an officer long employed in the fervice he defcribes. His own im-
provement was his principal motive in the compofition of them ; but being told that they might
convey many ufeful hints to others, and be of much fervice if laid before the public, he was pleafed
upon my requeft, freely to communicate them to me for that purpofe.

THE favages, thus fignally defeated in all their attempts to cut off this rein-forcement upon its march, began to retreat with the utmoft precipitation to their remote fettlements, wholly giving up their defigns againft Fort-Pitt; at which place Col. Bouquet arrived fafe with his convoy, four days after the ac-tion; receiving no further moleftation on the road, except a few fcattered fhot from a difheartened and flying enemy.

HERE the Colonel was obliged to put an end to the operations of this cam-paign, not having a fufficient force to purfue the enemy beyond the Ohio and take advantage of the victory obtained over them; nor having any reafon to expect a timely reinforcement from the provinces in their diftreffed fituation. He was therefore forced to content himfelf with fupplying Fort-Pitt, and other places on the communication, with provifions, ammunition, and ftores; ftationing his fmall army to the beft advantage he could, againft the approach of winter.

THE tranfactions of the fucceeding campaign, will be the fubject of the following work, and we fhall conclude this introduction, by fhewing the fenfe which his Majefty was pleafed to entertain, of the conduct and bravery of the officers and army, on this trying occafion.

HEAD-QUARTERS, NEW-YORK, Jan. 5, 1764.

ORDERS.

'HIS Majefty has been gracioufly pleafed to fignify to the commander in Chief, his royal approbation of the conduct and bravery of Col.
" BOUQUET, and the officers and troops under his command, in the two actions
" of the 5th and 6th of Auguft; in which, notwithftanding the many cir-
" cumftances of difficulty and diftrefs they laboured under, and the un-
" ufual fpirit and refolution of the Indians, they repelled and defeated the
" repeated attacks of the favages, and conducted their convoy fafe to Fort-
" Pitt."

Signed   MONCREIF,
Major of Brigade.

To Colonel BOUQUET,
or officer commanding at
Fort-Pitt.

Plate III

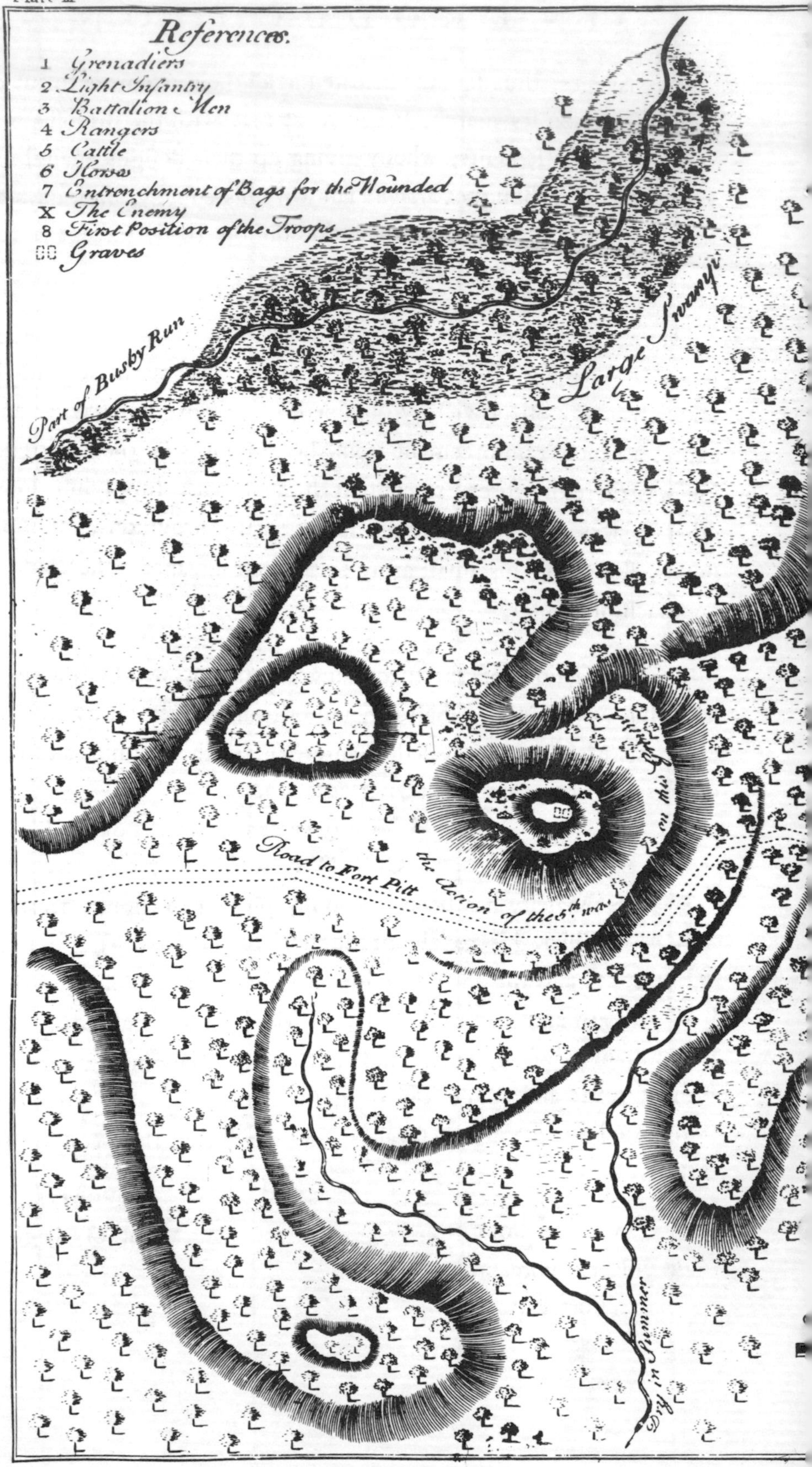

References.
1 Grenadiers
2 Light Infantry
3 Battalion Men
4 Rangers
5 Cattle
6 Horses
7 Entrenchment of Bags for the Wounded
X The Enemy
8 First Position of the Troops
⊟⊟ Graves

Part of Bushy Run

Large Swamp

Road to Fort Pitt

the Action of the 5th was

Dry in Summer

PLAN
of the
BATTLE near BUSHY=RUN
Gained by HIS MAJESTY'S Troops, commanded by
COLONEL HENRY BOUQUET
over the
DELAWARES, SHAWANESE, MINGOES,
WYANDOTS, MOHIKONS, MIAMIES & OTTAWAS,
on the 5.ᵗʰ and 6.ᵗʰ of August, 1763.
From an Actual Survey
By Thoˢ Hutchins
Assistant Engineer

Road from Fort Ligonier

Troops in Ambush

to support the Attack

Attack

Scale of Perches,
10   20   30   40   50   60

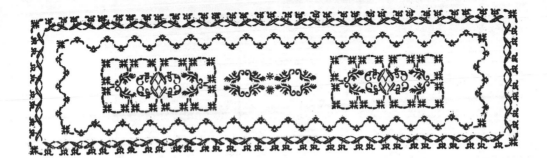

A N
HISTORICAL ACCOUNT
OF
Colonel Bouquet's Expedition,
Againſt the *Ohio* Indians in the Year 1764.

I N the preceeding introduction, ſome account hath been given of the ſudden, treacherous and unprovok'd attack, made by the Indians upon the frontiers of Pennſylvania, Maryland, and Virginia, ſoon after the publication of the general Peace, at a time when we were but juſt begining to reſpire from our former calamities, and looked for an approach of quiet on every ſide. The principal tranſactions of the campaign 1763 have likewiſe been briefly recapitulated, and the reader informed by what means the editor became poſſeſs'd of the valuable papers, which have enabled him to bring the hiſtory of this Indian war to a concluſion, and furniſhed the materials of the following ſheets.

COLONEL BOUQUET, as before mentioned, not having a ſufficient number of troops to garriſon the different poſts, under his command, and at the ſame time to croſs the Ohio and take advantage of the dejection into which he had thrown the enemy, by the defeat at Buſhy-Run, was obliged to reſtrain his

B

operations

operations to the fupplying the forts with provifions, ammunition and other neceffaries.

IN the execution of this fervice, he received no annoyance from the enemy, for they now faw themfelves not only forced to give up their defigns againft FORT-PITT; but, retreating beyond the Ohio, they deferted their former towns, and abandoned all the country between Prefque-Ifle and Sandufki; not thinking themfelves fafe till they arrived at Mufkingam.

HERE they began to form new fettlements, and remained quiet during the winter. But, in the mean time, having fupplied themfelves with powder &c. from the French traders, (and now flattering themfelves that the great diftance of their fettlements would render them inacceffible to our troops) the enfuing fpring 1764 prefented thefe favage enemies afrefh on our frontiers; ravaging and murdering with their ufual barbarity.

To chaftife them for their perfidy, General Gage refolved to attack them on two different fides, and to force them from our frontiers; by carrying the war into the heart of their own country. With this view, he deftined a corps of troops to proceed under Col. Bradftreet, to act againft the Wiandots, Ottawas, Chip-was and other nations, living upon or near the lakes; while another corps, under the command of Col. Bouquet fhould attack the Delawares, Shawa-nefe, Mingoes, Mohickons, and other nations, between the Ohio and the lakes.

THESE two corps were to act in concert; and as that of Col. Bradftreet could be ready much fooner than the other, he was to proceed to Detroit, Michili-mackinac and other places. On his return, he was to encamp and remain at Sandufki, to awe, by that pofition, the numerous tribes of weftern Indians, fo as to prevent their fending any affiftance to the Ohio Indians, while Colonel Bouquet fhould execute his plan of attacking them in the heart of their fettle-ments.

COL. BOUQUET'S expedition was to proceed altogether by land, and was on that account attended with great difficulties. His men were to penetrate thro'

a continued

a continued depth of woods, and a favage unexplor'd country; without roads, without pofts, and without a retreat if they failed of fuccefs. When once engaged in thefe deferts, they had no convoy, nor any kind of affiftance to expect. Every thing was to be carried with them----their ammunition, baggage, tools, ftores, and provifions neceffary for the troops during the whole expedition. And befides, they were liable to many embarrafments, and difficulties which no prudence could forefee, fcarce any caution prevent; fo that, in this account, fundry things, which, in the ufual method of conducting military operations might not be thought worthy of a detail, may neverthelefs be found highly ferviceable to thofe who may afterwards be employed in this fpecies of war, which is new to Europeans, who muft fubmit to be inftructed in it by experience, and in many articles even by the favages themfelves.

PART of the 42d and 60th regiments were ordered on this expedition, and were to be joined by two hundred friendly Indians, and the troops required of Virginia and Pennfylvania. The Indians never came, and the Virginians pleaded their inability to raife men, having already in pay about 700 militia for the defence of their own frontier. In Pennfylvania, a bill for raifing 1000 men was paffed May 30th; but, with the utmoft diligence that could be ufed, the number could not be compleated till the begining of Auguft.

ON the 5th of that month, the men being affembled at Carlifle, one hundred and eighteen miles to the weftward of Philadelphia, Governor Penn, who had accompanied Col. Bouquet to that place, acquainted the two Pennfylvania battalions with the neceffity we were laid under of chaftifing the Indians " for their repeated and unprovoked barbarities on the inhabitants of the pro-" vince; a juft refentment of which; added to a remembrance of the loyalty " and courage of our provincial troops on former occafions, he did not doubt, " would animate them to do honor to their country; and that they could not " but hope to be crown'd with fuccefs, as they were to be united with the " fame regular troops, and under the fame able commander, who had by them-" felves, on that very day, the memorable 5th of Auguft in the preceeding

" year, fuſtained the repeated attacks of the ſavages, and obtained a compleat
" victory over them."---He alſo reminded them " of the examplary puniſhments
" that would be inflicted on the grievous crime of deſertion, if any of them
" were capable of ſo far forgetting their ſolemn oath and duty to their king
" and country, as to be involved in it."

Col. Bouquet then aſſumed the command of the regular and provincial
troops; and the four following days were ſpent in the neceſſary preparations
for their march; the Colonel giving the moſt expreſs orders to the officers and
men to obſerve ſtrict diſcipline, and not to commit the leaſt violation of the
civil rights or peace of the inhabitants.---He, at the ſame time, made the
moſt prudent regulations for a ſafe and commodious carriage of the baggage,
taking care to rid himſelf of all unneceſſary incumbrances.

The 13th of Auguſt this ſmall army got to Fort Loudoun; but notwithſtanding all the precautions taken to prevent deſertion, the Pennſylvania
troops were now reduced to about 700 men.   The Colonel was therefore under a neceſſity to apply to the government of that province to enable him to
compleat their number to the full complement; which was generouſly granted by a reſolve of the Governor and Commiſſioners Auguſt 16th; and the
army advancing now beyond the ſettled parts of Pennſylvania, he made appli-
cation to the colony of Virginia, where (under the countenance of Governor Fauquier) the men wanted were ſoon raiſed, and joined the army at
Pittſburg, about the latter end of September.

Nothing material happened in their march, from Fort Loudoun to Fort
Pitt, (formerly Fort Du Queſne) on the Ohio, three hundred and twenty
miles weſt from Philadelphia; at which place Col. Bouquet arrived the 17th,
September.

During this interval, ſeveral large convoys were forwarded under ſtrong
eſcorts; and tho' the enemy continued their ravages all that time on the frontiers,

tiers, they durſt not attack any of thoſe convoys, which all arrived ſafe at Fort Pitt.

WHILE Col. Bouquet was at Fort Loudoun, he received diſpatches by expreſs from Col. Bradſtreet, dated from Preſque-Iſle Auguſt 14th, acquainting him that he (Col. Bradſtreet,) had concluded a peace with the Delawares and Shawaneſe ; but Col. Bouquet perceiving clearly that they were not ſincere in their intentions, as they continued their murders and depredations, he determined to proſecute his plan without remiſſion, till he ſhould receive further inſtructions from General Gage ; who, upon the ſame principles, refuſed to ratify the treaty, and renewed his orders to both armies to attack the enemy.

ABOUT the time of Col. Bouquet's arrival at Fort Pitt, ten Indians appeared on the north ſide of the Ohio, deſiring a conference ; which ſtratagem the ſavages had made uſe of before, to obtain intelligence of our numbers and intentions. Three of the party conſented, tho' with apparent reluctance, to come over to the Fort ; and as they could give no ſatisfactory reaſon for their viſit, they were detained as ſpies, and their aſſociates fled back to their towns.

ON the 20th of Sept. Col. Bouquet ſent one of the above three Indians after them with a meſſage, in ſubſtance as follows---- " I have received an account " from Col. Bradſtreet that your nations had begg'd for peace, which he had " conſented to grant, upon aſſurance that you had recalled all your warriors " from our frontiers ; and in conſequence thereof, I would not have proceed- " ed againſt your towns, if I had not heard that, in open violation of your en- " gagements, you have ſince murdered ſeveral of our people.

" As ſoon as the reſt of the army joins me, which I expect immediately, I was " therefore determined to have attacked you, as a people whoſe promiſes can no " more be relied on. But I will put it once more in your power to ſave your- " ſelves and your families from total deſtruction, by giving us ſatisfaction for " the hoſtilities committed againſt us. And firſt you are to leave the path

" open

" open for my expreffes from hence to Detroit; and as I am now to fend two
" men with difpatches to Col. Bradftreet who commands on the lakes, I defire
" to know whether you will fend two of your people with them to bring them
" fafe back with an anfwer? and if they receive any injury either in going or
" coming, or if the letters are taken from them, I will immediately put the
" Indians now in my power to death, and will fhew no mercy for the future
" to any of your nations that fhall fall into my hands. I allow you ten days
" to have my letters delivered at Detroit, and ten days to bring me back an
" anfwer."----

HE added " that he had lately had it in his power, while they remained on
" the other fide of the river, to have put their whole party to death, which
" punifhment they had deferved by their former treachery ; and that if they
" did not improve the clemency now offered to them, by returning back as
" foon as poffible with all their prifoners, they might expect to feel the full
" weight of a juft vengeance and refentment."---

WE have been the more particular in our account of this firft tranfaction
with the Indians ; becaufe the Colonel's firm and determined conduct in opening the campaign, had happy effects in the profecution of it, and fhews by
what methods thefe faithlefs favages are to be beft reduced to reafon.

ON the 1ft of October, two of the Six Nation tribes, an Onondago and
Oneida Indian, came to Fort Pitt, and under colour of our ancient friendfhip
with them, and their pretended regard to the Englifh, endeavoured to dif-
fuade the Colonel from proceeding with the army. They told him that his
force was not fufficient to withftand the power of the numerous nations
through whofe countries he was to pafs, and affured him that if he would
wait a little, they would all come and make peace with him ; at the fame time
recommending it particularly to him to fend back the two Indians detained
as fpies. Thefe little arts being clearly made ufe of to fpin out the feafon till
the approach of winter fhould render it impoffible to proceed, they made
but little impreffion. He told them that he could not depend on the pro-

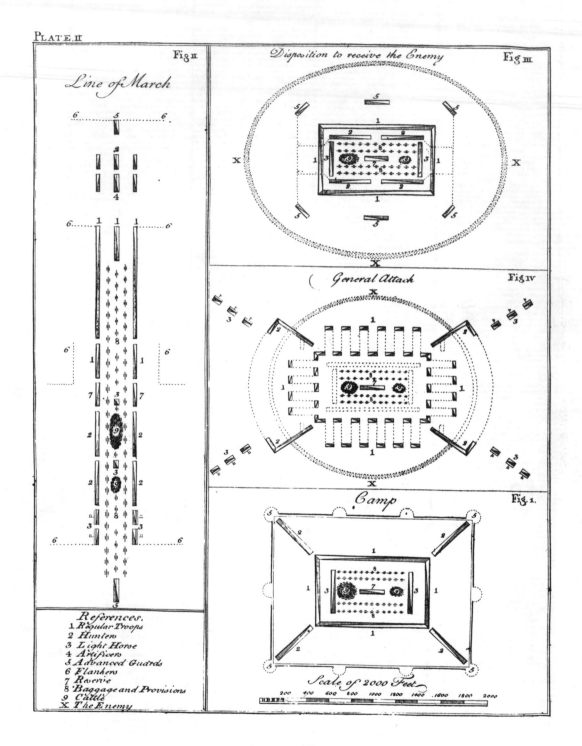

PLATE II

Fig II

Line of March

Disposition to receive the Enemy   Fig III

General Attack   Fig IV

Camp   Fig 1

References.
1 Regular Troops
2 Hunters
3 Light Horse
4 Artificers
5 Advanced Guards
6 Flankers
7 Reserve
8 Baggage and Provisions
9 Cattle
X The Enemy

Scale of 2000 Feet

200   400   600   800   1000   1200   1400   1600   1800   2000

miſes of the Delawares and Shawaneſe; and was determined to proceed to Tuſcarowas, where, if they had any thing to ſay, he would hear them.

In the mean time, he was uſing the utmoſt diligence to prepare for his march, and was obliged to enforce the ſevereſt diſcipline. One woman belonging to each corps, and two nurſes for the general hoſpital, were all that were permitted to follow the army. The other women in the camp, and thoſe unneceſſary in the garriſon, were ordered immediately down the country into the ſettlements. Two ſoldiers were ſhot for deſertion; an example which became abſolutely neceſſary to ſuppreſs a crime which, in ſuch an expedition, would have been attended with fatal conſequences, by weakening an army already too ſmall.

Col. Bouquet, having at length, with great difficulty, collected his troops, formed his magazines, and provided for the ſafety of the poſts he was to leave behind him, was ready on the 2d of October to proceed from Fort Pitt, with about 1500 men, including drivers and other neceſſary followers of the army.

As a juſt idea of the conduct of this expedition, and the great caution taken to prevent ſurprize, will be beſt obtained from the ORDER OF MARCH, we ſhall here inſert it, with a Copper Plate for the illuſtration of it, and an accurate Draught, taken from actual ſurveys, of the road and adjacent country, through which the army paſſed.

The Colonel, expreſſing the greateſt confidence in the bravery of the troops, told them, " he did not doubt but this war would ſoon be ended, under " God, to their own honor, and the future ſafety of their country, provided " the men were ſtrictly obedient to orders, and guarded againſt the ſurprizes " and ſudden attacks of a treacherous enemy, who never dared to face Britiſh " troops in an open field; that the diſtance of the enemy's towns, and the " clearing roads to them, muſt neceſſarily require a conſiderable time; that " the troops in thoſe deſerts, had no other ſupplies to expect but the ammunition.

" nition and provifions they carried with them; and that therefore the utmoft
" care and frugality would be neceffary in the ufe of them." He publifhed
the fevereft penalties againft thofe who fhould be found guilty of ftealing
or embezzling any part of them, and ordered his March in the following
manner.---

A corps of Virginia * volunteers advanced before the whole; detaching
three fcouting parties. One of them, furnifhed with a guide, marched in the
center path, which the army was to follow. The other two extended themfelves in a line a-breaft, on the right and left of the aforefaid party, to reco-
noitre the woods.

UNDER cover of this corps, the ax-men, confifting of all the artificers, and
two companies of light infantry, followed in three divifions, under the direction of the chief engineer, to clear three different paths, in which the
the troops and the convoy followed, viz.------

THE front-face of the fquare, compofed of part of the 42d. regiment,
marched in a column, two deep, in the center path.

THE right face of the fquare, compofed of the remainder of the 42d. and
of the 60th regiment, marched in a fingle file in the right hand path.

THE firft battalion of Pennfylvanians compofed the left face, marching in
like manner in the path to the left of the center.

THE corps de referve, compofed of two platoons of grenadiers, followed
the right and left faces of the fquare.

THE 2d battalion of Pennfylvanians formed the rear face of the fquare,
and followed the corps de referve, each in a fingle file, on the right and left
hand

* Thefe were the men raifed in Virginia to compleat the Pennfylvania troops, and were in the pay
of the laft mentioned province.

hand paths; all thefe troops covering the convoy, which moved in the center path.

A party of light horfe-men marched behind the rear-face of the fquare, followed by another corps of Virginia voluntiers, forming the rear-guard.

THE Pennfylvania volunteers, dividing themfelves equally, and marching in a fingle file, at a proper diftance, flanked the right and left faces of the fquare.

THIS was the general order of March. Nor was lefs attention paid to particular matters of a fubordinate nature. The ammunition and tools were placed in the rear of the firft column, or front face of the fquare, followed by the officer's baggage, and tents. The oxen and fheep came after the baggage, in feparate droves, properly guarded. The provifions came next to the baggage, in four divifions, or brigades of pack-horfes, each conducted by a horfe mafter.

THE troops were ordered to obferve the moft profound filence, and the men to march at two yards diftance from one another. When the line or any part of it halted, the whole were to face outwards; and if attacked on their march, they were to halt immediately, ready to form the fquare when ordered. The light horfe were then to march into the fquare, with the cattle, provifions, ammunition and baggage. Proper difpofitions were likewife made in cafe of an attack in the night; and for encampments, guards, communications between the centries, fignals, and the like.

THINGS being thus fettled, the army decamped from Fort-Pitt on Wednefday October 3d, and marched about one mile and an haf over a rich level country, with ftately timber, to camp No. 2. a ftrong piece of ground, pleafantly fituated, with plenty of water and food for cattle.

THURSDAY October 4th, having proceeded about two miles, they came to the Ohio, at the beginning of the narrows, and from thence followed the courfe

C of

courfe of the river along a flat gravelly beech, about fix miles and a quarter; with two iflands on their left, the lowermoft about fix miles long, with a rifing ground running acrofs, and gently floping on both fides to its banks, which are high and upright. At the lower end of this ifland, the army left the river, marching thro' good land, broken with fmall hollows to camp No .3; this day's march being nine miles and a quarter.----

FRIDAY October 5th. In this day's march, the army pafs'd thro' Loggs-town, fituated feventeen miles and an half, fifty feven perches, by the path, from Fort-Pitt. This place was noted before the laft war for the great trade carried on there by the Englifh and French; but its inhabitants, the Shawa-nefe and Delawares, abandoned it in the year 1750. The lower town extended about fixty perches over a rich bottom to the foot of a low fteep ridge, on the fummit of which, near the declivity, ftood the upper town, commanding a moft agreeable profpect over the lower, and quite acrofs the Ohio, which is a-bout five hundred yards wide here, and by its majeftic eafy current adds much to the beauty of the place. Proceeding beyond Loggs-town, thro' a fine country, interfperfed with hills and rich valleys, watered by many rivu-lets, and covered with ftately timber, they came to camp No. 4; on a level piece of ground, with a thicket in the rear, a fmall precipice round the front, with a run of water at the foot, and good food for cattle. This day's march was nine miles, one half, and fifty three perches.

SATURDAY October 6th, at about three miles diftance from this camp, they came again to the Ohio, purfuing its courfe half a mile farther, and then turn-ing off, over a fteep ridge, they crofs'd big Beaver-creek, which is twen-ty perches wide, the ford ftony and pretty deep. It runs thro' a rich vale, with a pretty ftrong current, its banks high, the upland adjoining it very good, the timber tall and young.----About a mile below its confluence with the Ohio, ftood formerly a large town, on a fteep bank, built by the French of fquare logs, with ftone chimneys, for fome of the Shawanefe, Delaware and Mingo tribes, who abandoned it in the year 1758, when the French deferted Fort Du Quefne. Near the fording of Beaver-creek alfo ftood about feven

houfes,

houfes, which were deferted and deftroyed by the Indians, after their defeat at Bufhy-run, when they forfook all their remaining fettlements in this part of the country, as has been mentioned above.

ABOUT two miles before the army came to Beaver-creek, one of our people who had been made prifoner by fix Delawares about a week before, near Fort Bedford, having made his efcape from them, came and informed the Colonel that thefe Indians had the day before fallen in with the army, but kept them-felves concealed, being furprized at our numbers. Two miles beyond Beaver-creek, by two fmall fprings, was feen the fcull of a child, that had been fixed on a pole by the Indians. The Tracts of 15 Indians were this day difcovered. The camp No. 5 is feven miles one quarter and fifty feven perches from big Beaver-creek; the whole march of this day being about twelve miles.

SUNDAY 7th October, paffing a high ridge, they had a fine profpect of an extenfive country to the right, which in general appeared level, with a-bundance of tall timber. The camp No. 6 lies at the foot of a fteep defcent, in a rich valley, on a ftrong ground, three fides thereof furrounded by a hollow, and on the fourth fide a fmall hill, which was occupied by a detached guard. This day's march was fix miles fixty five perches.

MONDAY 8th October, the army crofs'd little Beaver-creek, and one of ts branches. This creek is eight perches wide, with a good ford, the coun-try about it interfperfed with hills, rivulets and rich valleys, like that defcrib-ed above. Camp No. 7 lies by a fmall run on the fide of a hill, commanding the ground about it, and is diftant eleven miles one quarter and forty nine per-ches from the laft encampment.

TUESDAY October 9th. In this day's march, the path divided into two branches, that to the fouthweft leading to the lower towns upon the Mufking-ham. In the forks of the path ftand feveral trees painted by the Indians, in a hieroglyphic manner, denoting the number of wars in which they have been en-gag'd, and the particulars of their fuccefs in prifoners and fcalps. The camp

No. 8. lies on a run, and level piece of ground, with Yellow-creek close on the left, and a rifing ground near the rear of the right face. The path after the army left the forks was fo brufhy and entangled, that they were obliged to cut all the way before them, and alfo to lay feveral bridges, in order to make it paffable for the horfes ; fo that this day they proceeded only five miles, three quarters and feventy perches.

WEDNESDAY 10th. Marched one mile with Yellow-creek on the left at a fmall diftance all the way, and croffed it at a good ford fifty feet wide ; proceeding thro' an alternate fucceffion of fmall hills and rich vales, finely watered with rivulets, to camp No. 9. feven miles and fixty perches in the whole.

THURSDAY 11th. Crofs'd a branch of Mufkingham river about fifty feet wide, the country much the fame as that defcribed above, difcovering a good deal of free ftone. The camp No. 10. had this branch of the river parallel to its left face, and lies ten miles one quarter and forty perches from the former encampment.

FRIDAY 12th. Keeping the aforefaid creek on their left, they marched thro' much fine land, watered with fmall rivers and fprings ; proceeding likewife thro' feveral favannah's or cleared fpots, which are by nature extremely beautiful ; the fecond which they paffed being, in particular, one continued plain of near two miles, with a fine rifing ground forming a femicircle round the right hand fide, and a pleafant ftream of water at about a quarter of a mile diftant on the left. The camp No. 11. has the abovementioned branch of Mufkingham on the left, and is diftant ten miles and three quarters from the laft encampment.

SATURDAY 13th. Crofs'd Nemenfhehelas-creek, about fifty feet wide, a little above where it empties itfelf into the aforefaid branch of Mufkingham, having in their way a pleafant profpect over a large plain, for near two miles on the left. A little further, they came to another fmall river which they

crofs'd

cross'd about fifty perches above where it empties into the said branch of Muskingham. Here a high ridge on the right, and the creek close on the left, form a narrow defile about seventy perches long. Passing afterwards over a very rich bottom, they came to the main branch of Muskingham, about seventy yards wide, with a good ford. A little below and above the forks of this river is Tuscarowas, a place exceedingly beautiful by situation, the lands rich on both sides of the river; the country on the northwest side being an entire level plain, upwards of five miles in circumference. From the ruined houses appearing here, the Indians who inhabited the place and are now with the Delawares, are supposed to have had about one hundred and and fifty warriors. This camp No. 12. is distant eight miles nineteen perches from the former.

SUNDAY 14th. The army remained in camp; and two men who had been dispatched by Col. Bouquet from Fort-Pitt, with letters for Col. Bradstreet, returned and reported----" That, within a few miles of this place, they had been made prisoners by the Delawares, and carried to one of their towns sixteen miles from hence, where they were kept, till the savages, knowing of the arrival of the army here, set them at liberty, ordering them to acquaint the Colonel that the head men of the Delawares and Shawanese were coming as soon as possible to treat of peace with him."

MONDAY 15th. The army moved two miles forty perches further down the Muskingham to camp No. 13, situated on a very high bank, with the river at the foot of it, which is upwards of 100 yards wide at this place, with a fine level country at some distance from its banks, producing stately timber, free from underwood, and plenty of food for cattle.

THE day following, six Indians came to inform the Colonel that all their chiefs were assembled about eight miles from the camp, and were ready to treat with him of peace, which they were earnestly desirous of obtaining. He returned for answer that he would meet them the next day in a bower at some

distance

diftance from the camp. In the mean time, he ordered a fmall ftockaded fort to be built to depofit provifions for the ufe of the troops on their return ; and to lighten the convoy.

As feveral large bodies of Indians were now within a few miles of the camp, whofe former inftances of treachery, altho' they now declared they came for peace, made it prudent to truft nothing to their intentions, the ftricteft orders were repeated to prevent a furprife.

WEDNESDAY 17th. The Colonel, with moft of the regular troops, Virginia volunteers and light horfe, marched from the camp to the bower erected for the congrefs. And foon after the troops were ftationed, fo as to appear to the beft advantage, the Indians arrived, and were conducted to the bower. Being feated, they began, in a fhort time, to fmoak their pipe or calumet, a-agreable to their cuftom. This ceremony being over, their fpeakers laid down their pipes, and opened their pouches, wherein were their ftrings and belts of wampum. The Indians prefent were,

SENECAS.	DELAWARES.	SHAWANESE.
Kiyafhuta, chief with 15 warriors.	Cuftaloga, chief of the Wolfe-tribe, Beaver, chief of the Turky-tribe, with 20 warriors.	Keiffinautchtha, a chief, and 6 warriors.

Kiyafhuta, Turtle-Heart, Cuftaloga and Beaver, were the fpeakers.

The general fubftance of what they had to offer, confifted in excufes for their late treachery and mifconduct, throwing the blame on the rafhnefs of their young men and the nations living to the weftward of them, fuing for peace in the moft abject manner, and promifing feverally to deliver up all their prifoners. After they had concluded, the Colonel promifed to give them an anfwer the next day, and then difmiffed them, the army returning to the camp---The badnefs of the weather, however, prevented his meeting them again till the 20th, when he fpoke to them in fubftance as follows, viz.

" THAT their pretences to palliate their guilt by throwing the blame on the " weftern nations, and the rafhnefs of their young men, were weak and fri-
volous,

" volous, as it was in our power to have protected them againſt all theſe nati-
" ons, if they had ſollicited our aſſiſtance, and that it was their own duty to
" have chaſtiſed their young men when they did wrong, and not to ſuffer
" themſelves to be directed by them."

He recapitulated to them many inſtances of their former perfidy--- " their
" killing or captivating the traders who had been ſent among them at their
" own requeſt, and plundering their effects ;----their attacking Fort Pitt,
" which had been built with their expreſs conſent ; their murdering four
" men that had been ſent on a public meſſage to them, thereby violat-
" ing the cuſtoms held ſacred among all nations, however barbarous ; ----their
" attacking the king's troops laſt year in the woods, and after being defeated
" in that attempt, falling upon our frontiers, where they had continued to
" murder our people to this day. &c."---

He told them how treacherouſly they had violated even their late engagements with Col. Bradſtreet, to whom they had promiſed to deliver up their priſoners by the 10th of September laſt, and to recall all their warriors from the
frontiers, which they had been ſo far from complying with, that the priſoners
ſtill remained in their cuſtody, and ſome of their people were even now continuing their depredations ; adding that theſe things which, he had mentioned, were
only " a ſmall part of their numberleſs murders and breaches of faith ; and that
" their conduct had always been equally perfidious.---You have, ſaid he, pro-
" miſed at every former treaty, as you do now, that you would deliver up all
" your priſoners, and have received every time, on that account, conſidera-
" ble preſents, but have never complied with that or any other engagement.
" I am now to tell you, therefore, that we will be no longer impoſed upon
" by your promiſes. This army ſhall not leave your country till you have
" fully complied with every condition that is to precede my treaty with you.

" I have brought with me the relations of the people you have maſſacred,
" or taken priſoners. They are impatient for revenge ; and it is with great
" difficulty that I can protect you againſt their juſt reſentment, which is
                                                    " only

" only reftrained by the affurances given them, that no peace fhall ever be
" concluded till you have given us full fatisfaction.----

" YOUR former allies, the Ottawas, Chipwas, Wyandots, and others, have
" made their peace with us. The Six Nations have joined us againft you.
" We now furround you, having poffeffion of all the waters of the Ohio, the
" Miffiffippi, the Miamis, and the lakes. All the French living in thofe
" parts are now fubjects to the king of Great-Britain, and dare no longer affift
" you. It is therefore in our power totally to extirpate you from being a
" people----But the Englifh are a merciful and generous nation, averfe to fhed
" the blood, even of their moft cruel enemies; and if it was poffible that you
" could convince us, that you fincerely repent of your paft perfidy, and that
" we could depend on your good behaviour for the future, you might yet
" hope for mercy and peace-----If I find that you faithfully execute the follow-
" ing preliminary conditions, I will not treat you with the feverity you
" deferve.

" I GIVE you twelve days from this date to deliver into my hands at Waka-
" tamake all the prifoners in your poffeffion, without any exception; En-
" glifhmen, Frenchmen, women and children; whether adopted in your
" tribes, married, or living amongft you under any denomination and pre-
" tence whatfoever; together with all negroes. And you are to furnifh the
" faid prifoners with cloathing, provifions, and horfes, to carry them to
" Fort Pitt.

" WHEN you have fully complied with thefe conditions, you fhall then
" know on what terms you may obtain the peace you fue for."----

THIS fpeech made an impreffion on the minds of the favages, which, it is
hoped, will not foon be eradicated. The firm and determined fpirit with which
the Colonel delivered himfelf, their confcioufnefs of the aggravated injuries
they had done us, and the view of the fame commander and army that had fo

feverely

ſeverely chaſtiſed them at Buſhy-Run the preceeding year, now advanced into the very heart of their remote ſettlements, after penetrating thro' wilder-neſſes which they had deemed impaſſible by regular troops---all theſe things contributed to bend the haughty temper of the ſavages to the loweſt degree of abaſement; ſo that even their ſpeeches ſeem to exhibit but few ſpecimens of that ſtrong and ferocious eloquence, which their inflexible ſpirit of indepen-dency has on former occaſions inſpired. And tho' it is not to be doubted, if an opportunity had offered, but they would have fallen upon our army with their uſual fierceneſs, yet when they ſaw the vigilance and ſpirit of our troops were ſuch, that they could neither be attacked nor ſurprized with any proſ-pect of ſucceſs, their ſpirits ſeemed to revolt from the one extreme of inſolent boldneſs, to the other of abject timidity. And happy will it be for them and for us, if the inſtances of our humanity and mercy, which they experienced in that critical ſituation, ſhall make as laſting impreſſions on their ſavage diſ-poſitions, as it is believed the inſtances of our bravery and power have done; ſo that they may come to unite, with their fear of the latter, a love of the former; and have their minds gradually opened, by ſuch examples, to the mild dictates of peace and civility.

The reader, it is to be hoped, will readily excuſe this digreſſion if it ſhould be thought one. I now reſume our narrative. The two Delaware chiefs, at the cloſe of their ſpeech on the 17th, delivered 18 white priſoners, and 83 ſmall ſticks, expreſſing the number of other priſoners which they had in their poſſeſſion, and promiſed to bring in as ſoon as poſſible. None of the Shawaneſe kings appeared at the congreſs, and Keiſſinautchtha their deputy de-clined ſpeaking until the Colonel had anſwered the Delawares, and then with a dejected ſullenneſs he promiſed, in behalf of his nation, that they would ſub-mit to the terms preſcribed to the other tribes.

The Colonel, however, determined to march farther into their country, knowing that the preſence of his army would be the beſt ſecurity for the per-formance of their promiſes; and required ſome of each nation to attend him in his march.

D   KIYASHUTA

Kiyashuta addreffed the feveral nations, before their departure, " defir-
" ing them to be ftrong in complying with their engagements, that they
" might wipe away the reproach of their former breach of faith, and convince
" their brothers the Englifh that they could fpeak the truth; adding that he
" would conduct the army to the place appointed for receiving the prifoners."

Monday October 22d. The army attended by the Indian deputies, marched nine miles to camp No. 14. croffing Margaret's creek about fifty feet
wide---- The day following, they proceeded fixteen miles one quarter and feventy feven perches farther to camp No. 15. and halted there one day.

Thursday 25. They marched fix miles, one half and fixteen perches to
camp No. 16, fituated within a mile of the Forks of Mufkingham; and
this place was fixed upon inftead of Wakautamike, as the moft central and
convenient place to receive the prifoners; for the principal Indian towns now
lay round them, diftant from feven to twenty miles; excepting only
the lower Shawanefe town fituated on Scioto river, which was about
eighty miles; fo that from this place the army had it in their power to awe all
the enemy's fettlements and deftroy their towns, if they fhould not punctually fulfil the engagements they had entered into.-----Four redoubts were
built here oppofite to the four angles of the camp; the ground in the front
was cleared, a ftore-houfe for the provifions erected, and likewife a houfe
to receive, and treat of peace with, the Indians, when they fhould return.

On Saturday 27th. A meffenger arrived from king Cuftaloga, informing
that he was on his way with his prifoners, and alfo a meffenger from the lower
Shawanefe towns of the like import. The Colonel however, having reafon to
fufpect the latter nation of backwardnefs, fent one of their own people, defiring
them---- " to be punctual as to the time fixed; to provide a fufficient quanti-
" ty of provifions to fubfift the prifoners; to bring the letters wrote to him laft
" winter by the French commandant at Fort Chartres, which fome of their
                                                    " people

" people had ſtopp'd ever ſince ;" adding that, " as their nation had ex-
" preſſed ſome uneaſineſs at our not ſhaking hands with them, they were to
" know that the Engliſh never took their enemies by the hand, before peace
" was finally concluded."

THE day following, the Shawaneſe meſſenger returned, ſaying that when
he had proceeded as far as Wakautamike, the chief of that town undertook to
proceed with the meſſage himſelf, and deſired the other to return and acquaint
the Engliſh that all his priſoners were ready, and he was going to the lower
towns to haſten theirs.

OCTOBER 28th. Peter the Caughnawaga chief, and 20 Indians of that nation
arrived from Sanduſki, with a letter from Colonel Bradſtreet, in anſwer to one
which Colonel Bouquet had ſent to him from Fort-P.tt, by two of the Indians
who firſt ſpoke to him in favour of the Shawaneſe, as hath been already mentioned. The ſubſtance of Colonel Bradſtreet's letter was " that he had ſettled
nothing with the Shawaneſe and Delawares, nor received any priſoners from
them.----That he had acquainted all the Indian nations, as far as the Ilinois,
the bay &c. with the inſtructions he had received from General Gage, re-
ſpecting the peace he had lately made ; that he had been in Sanduſki-lake
and up the river, as far as navigable for Indian canoes, for near a month ;
but that he found it impoſſible to ſtay longer in theſe parts ; abſolute neceſſity obliging him to turn off the other way, &c.

COL. BRADSTREET, without doubt, did all which circumſtances would permit, in his department; but his not being able to remain at Sanduſki agreeable to the original plan, till matters were finally ſettled with the Ohio Indians,
would have been an unfavourable incident, if Colonel Bouquet had not now
had the chiefs of ſundry tribes with him, and was ſo far advanced into the Indian country, that they thought it adviſeable to ſubmit to the conditions impoſed upon them.

THE Caughnawagas reported that the Indians on the lakes had delivered but few of their prisoners ; that the Ottawas had killed a great part of theirs, and the other nations had either done the same, or else kept them.

FROM this time to November 9th, was chiefly spent in sending and receiving messages to and from the Indian towns, relative to the prisoners, who were now coming into the camp one day after another in small parties, as the different nations arrived in whose possession they had been. The Colonel kept so stedfastly to this article of having every prisoner delivered, that when the Delaware kings, Beaver and Custaloga, had brought in all their's except twelve which they promised to bring in a few days, he refused to shake-hands or have the last talk with them, while a single captive remained among them.

By the 9th of November, most of the prisoners were arrived that could be expected this season, amounting to ‡ 206 in the whole; besides about 100 more in possession of the Shawanese, which they promised to deliver the following spring. Mr. Smallman, formerly a Major in the Pennsylvania troops, who had been taken last summer near Detroit by the Wyandots, and delivered to the Shawanese, was among the number of those whom they now brought in, and informed the Colonel that the reason of their not bringing the remainder of their prisoners, was that many of their principal men, to whom they belonged, were gone to trade with the French, and would not return for six weeks; but that every one of their nation who were at home, had either brought or sent theirs. He further said that, on the army's first coming into the country, it had been reported among the Shawanese that our intention was to destroy them all, on which they had resolved to kill their prisoners and fight us; that a French trader who was with them, and had many barrels of powder and ball, made them a present of the whole, as soon as they had come to this resolution; but that, happily for the poor captives, just as the Shawanese were preparing to execute this tragedy, they received the Colonel's message, informing them

that

‡ Virginians,) Males,   32, Pennsylvanians,) Males,   49, In all 206.
) Females & Children, 58.   ) Females & Children, 67.

that his intentions were only to receive the priſoners and to make peace with them on the ſame terms he ſhould give to the Delawares.

On this intelligence they ſuſpended their cruel purpoſe, and began to collect as many of the priſoners as they had power to deliver; but hearing immediately afterwards that one of our ſoldiers had been killed near the camp at Muſkingham, and that ſome of their nation were ſuſpected as guilty of the murder, they again imagined they would fall under our reſentment, and therefore determined once more to ſtand out againſt us. For which purpoſe, after having brought their priſoners as far as Wakautamike, where they heard this news, they collected them all into a field, and were going to kill them, when a ſecond expreſs providentially arrived from Col. Bouquet, who aſſured them that their nation was not even ſuſpected of having any concern in the aforeſaid murder; upon which they proceeded to the camp to deliver up the captives, who had thus twice ſo narrowly eſcaped becoming the victims of their barbarity.

On Friday, November 9th, the Colonel, attended by moſt of the principal officers, went to the conference-houſe. The Senecas and Delawares were firſt treated with. Kiyaſhuta and 10 warriors repreſented the former. Cuſtaloga and 20 warriors the latter.

Kiyashuta ſpoke---" With this ſtring of wampum, we wipe the tears from
" your eyes---we deliver you theſe 3 priſoners, which are the laſt of your fleſh
" and blood that remained among the Senecas and Cuſtaloga's tribe of Delawares
" we gather together and bury with this belt † all the bones of the people that
" have been killed during this unhappy war, which the Evil Spirit occaſioned
" among us. We cover the bones that have been buried, that they may be
" never more remembered----We again cover their place with leaves that it
" may be no more ſeen.-----As we have been long aſtray, and the path between
" you and us ſtopped, we extend this belt that it may be again cleared, and
" we may travel in peace to ſee our brethren as our anceſtors formerly did.
" While

---

† A belt or ſtring is always delivered when thus mentioned.

" While you hold it faft by one end, and we by the other, we fhall always be
" able to difcover any thing that may difturb our friendfhip."----

THE Colonel anfwered that " he had heard them with pleafure ; that he re-
" ceived thefe 3 laft prifoners they had to deliver, and joined in burying the
" bones of thofe who had fallen in the war, fo that their place might be no more
" known. The peace you afk for, you fhall now have. The king, my mafter
" and your father, has appointed me only to make war ; but he has other fer-
" vants who are employed in the work of peace. Sir William Johnfon is em-
" powered for that purpofe. To him you are to apply ; but before I give
" you leave to go, two things are to be fettled.

1. " As peace cannot be finally concluded here, you will deliver me two hof-
" tages for the Senecas, and two for Cuftaloga's tribe, to remain in our hands
" at Fort Pitt, as a fecurity, that you fhall commit no further hoftilities or vio-
" lence againft any of his majefty's fubjects ; and when the peace is concluded
" thefe hoftages fhall be delivered fafe back to you.

2. " The deputies you are to fend to Sir William Johnfon, muft be fully
" empowered to treat for your tribes, and you fhall engage to abide by what-
" ever they ftipulate. In that treaty, every thing concerning trade and other
" matters will be fettled by Sir William, to render the peace everlafting ; and
" the deputies you are to fend to him, as well as the hoftages to be delivered
" to me, are to be named and prefented to me for my approbation.----

THE Colonel, after promifing to deliver back two of their people,
Capt. Pipe, and Capt. John, whom he had detained at Port-Pitt, took
the chiefs by the hand for the firft time, which gave them great joy.

THE next conference was on November 10th, with the Turkey and Turtle
tribes of Delawares, King Beaver their chief and 30 warriors reprefenting the
former ; and Kelappama brother to their * chief with 25 warriors the latter.

The

---

* The chief of the Turtle tribe, for fome reafon chofe to abfent himfelf.

The Senecas and Cuftaloga's tribe of Delawares were alfo prefent. Their fpeech and the anfwer given, were much the fame as above ; excepting that the Colonel infifted on their delivering up an Englifhman, who had murdered one of our people on the frontiers and brought the fcalp to them ; and that they fhould appoint the fame number of deputies and deliver the fame number of hoftages, for each of their tribes, as had been ftipulated for Cuftaloga's tribe.

November 11. King Beaver prefented fix hoftages to remain with Col. Bouquet, and five deputies to treat with Sir William Johnfon, who were approved of. This day he acquainted the chiefs prefent that as he had great reafon to be diffatisfied with the conduct of Nettowhatways, the chief of the Turtle tribe who had not appeared, he therefore depofed him; and that tribe were to chufe and prefent another for his approbation. This they did a few days afterwards---- Smile not reader at this tranfaction ; for tho' it may not be attended with fo many fplendid and flattering circumftances to a commander, as the depofing an Eaft Indian Nabob or chief ; yet to penetrate into the wildernefses where thofe ftern Weft Indian Chieftains hold their fway, and to frown them from their throne, tho' but compofed of the unhewn log, will be found to require both refolution and firmnefs ; and their fubmitting to it clearly fhews to what degree of humiliation they were reduced.

But to proceed. The Shawanefe ftill remained to be treated with, and tho' this nation faw themfelves under the neceffity of yielding to the fame conditions with the other tribes, yet there had appeared a dilatorinefs and fullen haughtinefs in all their conduct, which rendered it very fufpicious.

The 12th of November was appointed for the conference with them ; which was managed on their part by Keiffinautchtha and Nimwha their chiefs, with the Red Hawke, Laviffimo, Benfivafica, Eweecunwee, Keigleighque, and 40 warriors ; the Caughnawaga, Seneca and Delaware chiefs, with about 60 warriors, being alfo prefent.

The Red Hawke was their fpeaker, and as he delivered himfelf with a ftrange mixture of fierce pride, and humble fubmiffion, I fhall add a paffage or two from his fpeech.

BROTHER,

" You will liften to us your younger brothers; and as we difcover fome-
" thing in your eyes that looks diffatisfaction with us, we now wipe away
" every thing bad between us that you may clearly fee----You have heard
" many bad ftories of us----We clean your ears that you may hear----We re-
" move every thing bad from your heart, that it may be like the heart of
" your anceftors, when they thought of nothing but good." [Here he gave a ftring.]

" BROTHER; when we faw you coming this road, you advanced towards us
" with a Tomahawk in your hand; but we your younger brothers take it out
" of your hands and throw it up to God * to difpofe of as he pleafes; by which
" means we hope never to fee it more. And now brother, we beg leave
" that you who are a warrior, will take hold of this chain (giving a ftring) of
" friendfhip, and receive it from us, who are alfo warriors, and let us think
" no more of war, in pity to our old men, women and children"---Intimating,
by this laft expreffion, that it was mere compaffion to them, and not inability
to fight, that made their nation defire peace.

HE then produced a treaty held with the government of Pennfylvania 1701, and three meffages or letters from that government of different dates; and concluded thus.---

" Now Brother, I beg WE who are warriors may forget our difputes, and
" renew the friendfhip which appears by thefe papers to have fubfifted be-
" tween our fathers."-----He promifed, in behalf of the reft of their nation,
who were gone to a great diftance to hunt, and could not have notice to
attend the treaty, that they fhould certainly come to Fort-Pitt in the fpring,
and bring the remainder of the prifoners with them.

As

---

* Their ufual figure for making peace is burying the hatchet; but as fuch hatchets may be dug up again, perhaps he thought this new expreffion of " fending it up to God, or the Good Spirit," a much ftronger emblem of the permanency and ftedfaftnefs of the peace now to be made.

. As the ſeaſon was far advanced, and the Colonel could not ſtay long in theſe remote parts, he was obliged to reſt ſatisfied with the priſoners the Sha-waneſe had brought; taking hoſtages, and laying them under the ſtrongeſt obligations, for the delivery of the reſt; knowing that no other effectual method could at preſent be purſued.

He expoſtulated with them on account of their paſt conduct, and told them---- " that the ſpeech they had delivered would have been agreeable to
" him, if their actions had correſponded with their words. You have ſpoken,
" ſaid he, much of peace, but have neglected to comply with the only con-
" dition, upon which you can obtain it. Keiſſinautchtha, one of your chiefs,
" met me a month ago at Tuſcarawas, and accepted the ſame terms of peace
" for your nation, that were preſcribed to the Senecas and Delawares; pro-
" miſing in ten days from that time to meet me here with all your priſoners---
" After waiting for you till now, you are come at laſt, only with a part of them,
" and propoſe putting off the delivery of the reſt till the ſpring----What right
" have you to expect different terms from thoſe granted to the Delawares &c.
" who have given me entire ſatisfaction by their ready ſubmiſſion to every
" thing required of them?----But I will cut this matter ſhort with you; and
" before I explain myſelf further, I inſiſt on your immediate anſwer to the
" following queſtions."- -

1ſt. " Will you forthwith collect and deliver up all the priſoners yet in your
" poſſeſſion, and the French living among you, with all the Negroes you
" have taken from us in this or any other war; and that without any ex-
" ception or evaſion whatſoever?"

2d. " Will you deliver ſix hoſtages into my hands as a ſecurity for your
" punctual performance of the above article, and that your nations ſhall com-
" mit no farther hoſtilities againſt the perſons or property of his majeſty's
" ſubjects?"

Benevissico replyed that " they agreed to give the hoſtages required, and
" ſaid that he himſelf would immediately return to their lower towns and col-
E   " lect

" left all our flesh and blood that remained among them, and that we should
" see them at Fort-Pitt * as soon as possible.----That, as to the French, they
" had no power over them. They were subjects to the king of England. We
" might do with them what we pleased; tho' he believed they were all re-
" turned before this time to their own country"----

They then delivered their hostages, and the Colonel told them " that
" tho' he had brought a Tomahawk in his hand, yet as they had now submit-
" ted, he would not let it fall on their heads, but let it drop to the ground,
" no more to be seen. He exhorted them to exercise kindness to the captives,
" and look upon them now as brothers and no longer prisoners; adding that he
" intended to send some of their relations along with the Indians, to see their
" friends collected and brought to Fort-Pitt. He promised to give them letters
" to Sir William Johnson, to facilitate a final peace, and desired them to be
" strong in performing every thing stipulated."

The Caughnawagas, the Delawares and Senecas, severally addressed the Shawanese, as grand children and nephews, " to perform their promises, and to
" be strong in doing good, that this peace might be everlasting."-----

And here I am to enter on a scene, reserved on purpose for this place, that
the thread of the foregoing narrative might not be interrupted---a scene, which
language indeed can but weakly describe; and to which the Poet or Painter
might have repaired to enrich their highest colorings of the variety of human
passions; the Philosopher to find ample subject for his most serious reflections;
and the Man to exercise all the tender and sympathetic feelings of the soul.

The scene, I mean, was the arrival of the prisoners in the camp; where were
to be seen fathers and mothers recognizing and clasping their once-lost babes;
husbands hanging round the necks of their newly-recovered wives; sisters and
brothers unexpectedly meeting together after long separation, scarce able to
speak the same language, or, for some time, to be sure that they were children
of the same parents! In all these interviews, joy and rapture inexpressible were

                                                                    seen

---

* It will appear, by the postscript to this account, that the Shawanese have fulfilled this engagement.

feen, while feelings of a very different nature were painted in the looks of others;----flying from place to place in eager enquiries after relatives not found! trembling to receive an anfwer to their queftions! diftracted with doubts, hopes and fears, on obtaining no account of thofe they fought for! or ftiffened into living monuments of horror and woe, on learning their unhappy fate!

THE Indians too, as if wholly forgetting their ufual favagenefs, bore a capital part in heightning this moft affecting fcene. They delivered up their beloved captives with the utmoft reluctance; fhed torrents of tears over them, recommending them to the care and protection of the commanding officer. Their regard to them continued all the time they remained in camp. They vifited them from day to day; and brought them what corn, fkins, horfes and other matters, they had beftowed on them, while in their families; accompanied with other prefents, and all the marks of the moft fincere and tender affection. Nay, they did not ftop here, but, when the army marched, fome of the Indians follicited and obtained leave to accompany their former captives all the way to Fort-Pitt, and employed themfelves in hunting and bringing provifions for them on the road. A young Mingo carried this ftill further, and gave an inftance of love which would make a figure even in romance. A young woman of Virginia was among the captives, to whom he had form'd fo ftrong an attachment, as to call her his wife. Againft all remonftrances of the imminent danger to which he expofed himfelf by approaching to the frontiers, he perfifted in following her, at the rifk of being killed by the furviving relations of many unfortunate perfons, who had been captivated or fcalped by thofe of his nation.

THOSE qualities in favages challenge our juft efteem. They fhould make us charitably confider their barbarities as the effects of wrong education, and falfe notions of bravery and heroifm; while we fhould look on their virtues as fure marks that nature has made them fit fubjects of cultivation as well as us; and that we are called by our fuperior advantages to yield them all the helps we can in this way. Cruel and unmerciful as they are, by habit and long example, in war, yet whenever they come to give way to the native dictates of humanity, they exercife virtues which Chriftians need not blufh to imitate.

        When

When they once determine to give life, they give every thing with it, which, in their apprehenfion, belongs to it. From every enquiry that has been made, it appears---that no woman thus faved is preferved from bafe motives, or need fear the violation of her honor. No child is otherwife treated by the perfons adopting it than the children of their own body. The perpetual flavery of thofe captivated in war, is a notion which even their barbarity has not yet fuggefted to them. Every captive whom their affection, their caprice, or whatever elfe, leads them to fave, is foon incorporated with them, and fares alike with themfelves.

THESE inftances of Indian tendernefs and humanity were thought worthy of particular notice. The like inftances among our own people will not feem ftrange; and therefore I fhall only mention one, out of a multitude that might be given on this occafion.

AMONG the captives, a woman was brought into the camp at Mufkingham, with a babe about three months old at her breaft. One of the Virginia-volunteers foon knew her to be his wife, who had been taken by the Indians about fix months before. She was immediately delivered to her overjoyed hufband. He flew with her to his tent, and cloathed her and his child in proper apparel. But their joy, after the firft tranfports, was foon damped by the reflection that another dear child of about two years old, captivated with the mother, and feparated from her, was ftill miffing, although many children had been brought in.

A FEW days afterwards, a number of other prifoners were brought to the camp, among whom were feveral more children. The woman was fent for, and one, fuppofed to be hers, was produced to her. At firft fight fhe was uncertain, but viewing the child with great earneftnefs, fhe foon recollected its features; and was fo overcome with joy, that literally forgetting her fucking child fhe dropt it from her arms, and catching up the new found child in an extafy, preffed it to her breaft, and burfting into tears carried it off, unable to fpeak for joy. The father feizing up the babe fhe had let fall, followed her in no lefs tranfport and affection.

AMONG

AMONG the children who had been carried off young, and had long lived with the Indians, it is not to be expected that any marks of joy would appear on being reſtored to their parents or relatives. Having been accuſtomed to look upon the Indians as the only connexions they had, having been tenderly treated by them, and ſpeaking their language, it is no wonder that they conſidered their new ſtate in the light of a captivity, and parted from the ſavages with tears.

BUT it muſt not be denied that there were even ſome grown perſons who ſhewed an unwillingneſs to return. The Shawaneſe were obliged to bind ſeveral of their priſoners and force them along to the camp ; and ſome women, who had been delivered up, afterwards found means to eſcape and run back to the Indian towns. Some, who could not make their eſcape, clung to their ſavage acquaintance at parting, and continued many days in bitter lamentations, even refuſing ſuſtenance.

FOR the honor of humanity, we would ſuppoſe thoſe perſons to have been of the loweſt rank, either bred up in ignorance and diſtreſſing penury, or who had lived ſo long with the Indians as to forget all their former connexions. For, eaſy and unconſtrained as the ſavage life is, certainly it could never be put in competiton with the bleſſings of improved life and the light of religion, by any perſons who have had the happineſs of enjoying, and the capacity of diſcerning, them.

EVERY thing being now ſettled with the Indians, the army decamped on Sunday 18th November, and marched for Fort-Pitt, where it arrived on the 28th. The regular troops were immediately ſent to garriſon the different poſts on the communication, and the provincial troops, with the captives, to their ſeveral provinces. Here ended this expedition, in which it is remarkable that, notwithſtanding the many difficulties attending it, the troops were never in want of any neceſſaries ; continuing perfectly healthy during the whole campaign; in which no life was loſt, except the man mentioned to have been killed at Muſkingham.

IN

IN the beginning of January 1765, Colonel Bouquet arrived at Philadelphia, receiving, wherever he came, every poffible mark of gratitude and efteem from the people in general; and particularly from the overjoyed relations of the captives, whom he had fo happily, and without bloodfhed, reftored to their country and friends. Nor was the legiflative part of the provinces lefs fenfible of his important fervices. The affembly of Pennfylvania, at their firft fitting, unanimoufly voted him the following addrefs.

In A S S E M B L Y, January 15, 1765, A. M.
To the H O N O R A B L E
H E N R Y   B O U Q U E T, Efq;
Commander in Chief of His M A J E S T Y's Forces in the Southern Department of A M E R I C A,

The A D D R E S S of the R E P R E S E N T A T I V E S of the FREEMEN of the province of Pennfylvania, in GENERAL ASSEMBLY met.

S I R,

' T H E reprefentatives of the freemen of the province of Pennfylva-
        nia, in general affembly met, being informed that you intend
' fhortly to embark for England, and moved with a due fenfe of the im-
' portant fervices you have rendered to his majefty, his northern colonies in
' general, and to this province in particular, during our late wars with the
' French and barbarous Indians, in the remarkable victory over the favage
' enemy, united to oppofe you, near Bufhy-Run, in Auguft 1763, when on
' your March for the relief of Pittfburg, owing, under God, to your intrepidy
' and fuperior fkill in command, together with the bravery of your officers
' and little army ; as alfo in your late march to the country of the favage nati-
' ons, with the troops under your direction ; thereby ftriking terror through
' the numerous Indian tribes around you ; laying a foundation for a lafting as
' well as honorable peace with them ; and refcuing, from favage captivity,
' upwards of two hundred of our chriftian brethren, prifoners among them :
' thefe eminent fervices, and your conftant attention to the civil rights of his
' majefty's fubjects in this province, demand, Sir, the grateful tribute of
' thanks from all good men ; and therefore we, the reprefentatives of the free-

' men

' men of Pennfylvania, unanimoufly for ourfelves, and in behalf of all the
' people of this province, do return you our moft fincere and hearty thanks for
' thefe your great fervices, wifhing you a fafe and pleafant voyage to England,
' with a kind and gracious reception from his majefty.

Signed, by order of the Houfe,
J O S E P H   F O X, Speaker.

The Colonel's anfwer was as follows, viz.

To the Honorable the REPRESENTATIVES of the Freemen of the province of Pennfylvania, in General-Affembly met.

     Gentlemen,

' WITH a heart impreffed with the moft lively fenfe of gratitude, I return you my humble and fincere thanks, for the honor you
' have done me in your polite Addrefs of the 15th of January, tranfmitted me
' to New-York by your fpeaker.

' Next to the approbation of His Sacred Majefty, and my fuperior
' officers, nothing could afford me higher pleafure than your favourable opi-
' nion of my conduct, in the difcharge of thofe military commands with
' which I have been intrufted.

' Gratitude as well as juftice demand of me to acknowledge, that the
' aids granted by the legiflature of this province, and the conftant affiftance
' and fupport afforded me by the honourable the Governor and Commiffioners
' in the late expedition, have enabled me to recover fo many of his Majef-
' ty's fubjects from a cruel captivity, and be the happy inftrument of re-
' ftoring them to freedom and liberty: To you therefore, gentlemen, is the
' greater fhare of that merit due, which you are generoufly pleafed on this
' occafion to impute to my fervices.

' Your kind teftimony of my conftant attention to the civil rights of his
' majefty's fubjects in this Province, does me fingular honour, and calls for
' the return of my warmeft acknowledgments.

Permit

' Permit me to take this public opportunity of doing justice to the offi-
' cers of the regular and provincial troops, and the volunteers, who have
' served with me, by declaring that, under Divine Providence, the repeated
' successes of his Majesty's arms against a savage enemy, are principally to
' be ascribed to their courage and resolution, and to their perseverance under
' the severest hardships and fatigue.

' I sincerely wish prosperity and happiness to the province, and have
' the honour to be, with the greatest respect, Gentlemen,

Your most obedient, and most humble servant,

HENRY BOUQUET.

February 4, 1765.

Soon afterwards the Colonel received a very polite and affectionate letter
from Governor Fauquier, dated 25th of December, enclosing Resolves of the
honorable members of his Majesty's Council, and of the house of Burgesses,
for the colony and dominion of Virginia.

Those respectable bodies unanimously returned their thanks to him for
the activity, spirit and zeal, with which he had reduced the Indians to terms
of peace, and compelled those savages to deliver up so many of his Majesty's
subjects whom they had in captivity. They further requested the Governor
to recommend him to his Majesty's ministers, as an officer of distinguished
merit, in this and every former service in which he has been engaged.

The Colonel, in his answer, acknowledged the ready assistance and countenance which he had always received from the Governor and colony of Virginia in carrying on the King's service; and mentioned his particular obligations to Col. Lewis, for his zeal and good conduct during the campaign.

The honors thus bestowed on him, his own modesty made him desirous of transfering to the officers and army under his command; and indeed the mutual confidence and harmony subsisting between him and them,

highly

highly redound to the reputation of both. He has taken every occasion of doing juftice to the particular merit of Col. REID who was fecond in command; and alfo to all the officers who ferved in the expedition, regulars as well as * provincials.

THE reader will obferve that the public. bodies who prefented thefe addreffes to the Colonel, not only wifhed to exprefs their own gratitude, but likewife to be inftrumental in recommending him to the advancement·his fervices merited. And furely it is a happy circumftance to obtain promotion, not only unenvied, but even with the general approbation and good wifhes of the public. It ought, however, to be mentioned, that on the firft account his Majefty received of this expedition, and long before thofe teftimonies could reach England, he was gracioufly pleafed, of his own royal goodnefs and as a reward of the Colonel's merit, to promote him to the rank of BRIGADIER GENERAL, and to the command of the fouthern diftrict of America. And as he is rendered as dear, by his private virtues, to thofe who have the honour of his more intimate acquaintance, as he is by his military fervices to the public, it is hoped he may long continue among us; where his experienced abilities will enable him, and his love of the Englifh conftitution entitle him, to fill any future truft to which his Majefty may be pleafed to call him.————

❀❀❀❀❀❀❀❀❀❀❀❀❀❀ ❀❀❀❀❀❀❀❀❀❀❀❀❀❀❀❀❀❀

POSTSCRIPT.

T was mentioned in the 25th page of this account, that the Shawanefe brought only a part of their prifoners with them to Col. Bouquet at Mufkingham, in November laft; and that, as the feafon was far advanced, he was obliged to reft fatisfied with taking hoftages for the delivery of the remainder at Fort-Pitt, in the enfuing fpring.

F

THE

* The Pennfylvania troops were commanded by Lieutenant Colonel Francis, and Lieutenant Colonel Clayton.

THE escape of those hostages soon afterwards; as well as the former equivocal conduct of their nation, had given reason to doubt the sincerity of their intentions with respect to the performance of their promises. But we have the satisfaction to find that they punctually have fulfilled them. Ten of their chiefs, and about 50 of their warriors, attended with many of their women and children, met GEORGE CROGHAN, Esq; deputy agent to Sir WILLIAM JOHNSON, at Fort-Pitt the 9th of last May; together with a large body of Delawares, Senecas, Sandusky and Munsy Indians; where they delivered the remainder of their prisoners, brightened the chain of friendship, and gave every assurance of their firm intentions to preserve the Peace inviolable for ever.

THERE is something remarkable in the appellation they gave to the English on this occasion; calling them Fathers instead of Brethren.

LAWAUGHQUA, the Shawanese speaker, delivered himself in the following terms.----

" FATHERS, for so we will call you henceforward; listen to what we are
" going to say to you.

" IT gave us great pleasure yesterday to be called the children of the great
" King of England; and convinces us your intentions towards us are upright,
" as we know a Father will be tender of his children, and they are more rea-
" dy to obey him than a Brother. Therefore we hope our Father will now
" take better care of his children, than has heretofore been done. ---

You put us in mind of our promise to Col. Bouquet; which was to bring
" your flesh and blood to be delivered at this place. FATHER, you have not
" spoke in vain---you see we have brought them with us,----except a few that
" were out with our hunting parties, which will be brought here as soon as
" they return.

" THEY have been all united to us by adoption; and altho' we now deli-
" ver them up to you, we will always look upon them as our relations,
" whenever the Great Spirit is pleased that we may visit them.

" FATHER

" FATHER, We have taken as much care of them, as if they were our own
" flesh and blood. They are now become unacquainted with your customs
" and manners; and therefore, we request you will use them tenderly and
" kindly, which will induce them to live contentedly with you.

" HERE is a belt with the figure of our Father the King of Great-Britain
" at one end, and the Chief of our nation at the other. It represents them
" holding the chain of friendship; and we hope neither side will slip their
" hands from it, so long as the Sun and Moon give light."

THE reader will further remember that one of the engagements which the
different Indian Tribes entered into with Colonel Bouquet, was to send deputies to conclude a peace with Sir WILLIAM JOHNSON. This has also
been punctually fulfilled; and we are assured that Sir WILLIAM " has finish-
" ed his congress greatly to his satisfaction, and even beyond his expectati-
" ons." Thus every good consequence has ensued from this important
expedition, which our fondest wishes could have induced us to expect from
the known valor and spirit of the able Commander who had the conduct of it;
and we now have the pleasure once more to behold the temple of JANUS shut,
in this western world!

REFLECTIONS

ON THE

WAR

WITH THE

Savages of *North-America.*

T HE long continued ravages of the Indians on the frontiers of the British colonies in America, and the fatal overthrows which they have sometimes given our best disciplined troops, especially in the beginning of the late war, have rendered them an object of our consideration, even in their military capacity. And as but few officers, who may be employed against them, can have opportunities to observe the true causes of their advantages over European troops in the woods, it is with the utmost pleasure that I now proceed to lay before the public the following valuable papers, which I mentioned * to have been communicated to me by an officer of great abilities and long experience, in our wars with the Indians.

As scarce any thing has yet been published on a subject now become of the highest importance § to our colonies, these papers will undoubtedly be an acceptable present to the reader; and the remarks contained in them may be more and more improved by the future care and attention of able men, till perhaps a compleat system is at length formed for the conduct of this particular species of war.

SECTION

* See the introduction.
§ It will appear by the account of Indian tribes and towns annexed to these papers, that the enemies we have to deal with are neither contemptible in numbers or strength.

S E C T I O N I.

OF THE TEMPER AND GENIUS OF THE INDIANS.

THE love of liberty is innate in the favage; and feems the ruling paffion of the ftate of nature. His defires and wants being few are eafily gratified, and leave him much time to fpare, which he would fpend in idlenefs, if hunger did not force him to hunt. That exercife makes him ftrong, active and bold, raifes his courage, and fits him for war, in which he ufes the fame ftratagems and cruelty as againft the wild beafts; making no fcruple to employ treachery and perfidy to vanquifh his enemy.

JEALOUS of his independency and of his property, he will not fuffer the leaft encroachment on either; and upon the flighteft fufpicion, fired with refentment, he becomes an implacable enemy, and flies to arms to vindicate his right, or revenge an injury.

THE advantages of thefe favages over civilized nations are both natural and acquired. They are tall and well limbed, remarkable for their activity, and have a peircing eye and quick ear, which are of great fervice to them in the woods.

LIKE beafts of prey, they are patient, deceitful, and rendered by habit almoft infenfible to the common feelings of humanity. Their barbarous cuftom of fcalping their enemies, in the heat of action; the exquifite torments often inflicted by them on thofe referved for a more deliberate fate; their general ferocity of manners, and the fucceffes wherewith they have often been flufh'd, have confpired to render their name terrible, and fome times to ftrike a pannic even into our braveft and beft difciplined troops.

THEIR acquired advantages are, that they have been inured to bear the extremes of heat and cold; and from their infancy, in Winter and Summer, to plunge themfelves in cold ftreams, and to go almoft naked, expofed to the fcorching fun or nipping frofts, till they arrive to the ftate of manhood. Some of them deftroy the fenfation of the fkin by fcratching it with the fhort and

fharp

sharp teeth of some animal, disposed in the form of a curry-comb, which makes them regardless of briars and thorns in running thro' thickets. Rivers are no obstacles to them in their wild excursions. They either swim over, or cross them on rafts or canoes, of an easy and ready construction.

In their expeditions they live chiefly by hunting, or on wild fruits and roots, with which the woods supply them almost every where.

They can bear hunger and thirst for several days, without slackening, on that account, their perseverance in any proposed enterprize.

By constant practice in hunting, they learn to shoot with great skill, either with bows, or fire arms; and to steal unperceived upon their prey, pursuing the tracts of men and beasts, which would be imperceptible to an European. They can run for a whole day without halting, when flying from an enemy, or when sent on any message. They steer, as if by instinct, thro' trackless woods, and with astonishing patience can lie whole days motionless in ambush to surprize an enemy, esteeming no labour or perseverance too painful to obtain their ends.

They besmear their bodies with Bear's grease, which defends them against rains and damps, as well as against the stings of Muskitoes and Gnats. It likewise supples their limbs, and makes them as slippery as the antient Gladiators, who could not be held fast when seized in fight.

Plain food, constant exercise, and living in the open air, preserve them healthy and vigorous.

They are powerfully excited to war by the custom established among them, of paying distinguished honors to Warriors.

They fight only when they think to have the advantage, but cannot be forced to it, being sure by their speed to elude the most eager pursuit.

Their

THEIR drefs confift of the fkins of fome wild beaft, or a blanket, a fhirt either of linen, or of dreffed fkins, a breech clout, leggins, reaching half way up the thigh, and faftened to a belt, with mokawfons on their feet. They ufe no ligatures that might obftruct the circulation of their blood, or agility of their limbs. They fhave their head, referving only a fmall tuft of hair on the top; and flit the outer part of the ears, to which, by weights, they give a circular form, extending it down to their fhoulders.

THEY adorn themfelves with ear and nofe rings, bracelets of filver and wampum, and paint their faces with various colours. When they prepare for an engagement they paint themfelves black, and fight naked.

THEIR arms are a fufil, or rifle, a powder horn, a fhot pouch, a toma-hawk, and a fcalping knife hanging to their neck.

WHEN they are in want of fire arms, they fupply them by a bow, a fpear, or a death hammer, which is a fhort club made of hard wood.

THEIR ufual utenfils are a kettle, a fpoon, a looking glafs, an awl, a fteel to ftrike fire, fome paint, a pipe and tobacco pouch. For want of tobacco, they fmoke fome particular leaves, or the bark of a willow; which is almoft their continual occupation.

THUS lightly equiped do the favages lie in wait to attack, at fome difficult pafs, the European foldier, heavily accoutred, harraffed by a tedious march, and encumbered with an unwieldy convoy.

EXPERIENCE has convinced us that it is not our intereft to be at war with them; but if after having tried all means to avoid it, they force us to it, (which in all probability will often happen) we fhould endeavour to fight them upon more equal terms, and regulate our Manœuvres upon thofe of the enemy we are to engage, and the nature of the country we are to act in.

IT does not appear from our accounts of Indian wars, that the favages were as brave formerly as we have found them of late; which muft be imputed

to

to their unexpected fucceffes againft our troops on fome occafions, particularly in 1755; and from the little refiftance they have fince met with from defencelefs inhabitants.

It is certain that even at this day, they feldom expofe their perfons to danger, and depend entirely upon their dexterity in concealing themfelves during an engagement, never appearing openly, unlefs they have ftruck their enemies with terror, and have thereby rendered them incapable of defence.---- From whence it may be inferred that, if they were beat two or three times, they would lofe that confidence infpired by fuccefs, and be lefs inclined to engage in wars which might end fatally for them. But this cannot reafonably be expected, till we have troops trained to fight them in their own way, with the additional advantage of European courage and difcipline.

Any deviation from our eftablifhed military fyftem would be needlefs, if valor, zeal, order and good conduct, were fufficient to fubdue this light-footed enemy. Thefe qualities are confpicuous in our troops; but they are too heavy, and indeed too valuable, to be employed alone in a deftructive fervice for which they were never intended. They require the affiftance of lighter corps, whofe drefs, arms and exercifes, fhould be adapted to this new kind of war.

This opinion is fupported by the example of many warlike nations, of which I beg leave to mention the following.

The learned * Jefuit who has obliged the world with a treatife on the militay affairs of the ancient Romans, tells us from § Salluft that this wife nation, our mafters in the art of war, were never hindered even by the pride of empire, from imitating any foreign maxim or inftitution, provided it was good; and that they carefully adopted into their own practice whatever they found ufeful in that of their allies or enemies; fo that by receiving fome things from one, and fome from another, they greatly improved a fyftem even originally excellent.

G   The

* Vid. Joannis Antonii Valtrini Lbr. de re milit. Vet. Rom.

§ Neque enim Romanis fuperbia unquam obftitit, quo minus aliena inftituta, fi modo proba fuiffent, imitarentur ; et quod ubique apud focios vel hoftes idoneum vifum effet, cum ftudio domi exfequerentur---Aliaque ab aliis accepta, ipfi longe facere meliora quæ quidem digna ftatuiffent.

The defeat of Antony and Craffus by the Parthians, of Curio by the Numidians, and many other inftances, convinced the Romans that their legions, who had conquered fo many nations, were not fit to engage light-troops, which, harraffing them continually, evaded all their endeavours to bring them to a clofe engagement; and it is probable that if Julius Cæfar had not been affaffinated, when he was preparing to march againft the fame Parthians, to wipe off the reproach of the former defeats, he would have added to his legions a greater number of light troops, formed upon the principles and method of that nation, and have left us ufeful leffons for the conduct of a war againft our favages.

That he did not think the attack of irregular troops contemptible, appears clearly in feveral parts of his commentaries, and particularly in the African war. The various embarrafments he met with from the enemy he had then to deal with, neceffarily call to our mind many fimilar circumftances in the courfe of our wars with the Indians; and the pains he took to inftruct his foldiers to ftand and repel the fkirmifhes of the nimble Africans, may furnifh inftruction to us in our military operations againft the favage Americans.

We are told that while Cæfar was on his march " to Scipio's * quarters, the " enemy's horfe and light armed Infantry, rifing all at once from an ambuf-" cade, appeared upon the hills, and attacked his rear. His legions forming " themfelves, foon beat the enemy from the higher ground. And now think-" ing all fafe, he begins to purfue his march. But immediately the enemy " break forth from the neighbouring hills; and the Numidians, with their
" light

---

* Labienus, Afraniufque cum omni equitatu, levique armatura, ex infidiis adorti agmini Cæfaris extremo fe offerunt, atque ex collibus primis exfiftunt.- -Primo impetu legionum equitatus, levis armatura hoftium nullo negotio loco pulfa et dejecta eft de colle. Quum jam Cæfar exiftimaffet hoftes pulfos deterritofque finem laceffendi facturos, et iter cœptum pergere cœpiffet; iterum celeritur ex proximis collibus erumpunt; atque in Cæfaris legionarios impetum faciunt Numidæ, levifque armaturæ, mirabili velocitate præditi; qui inter equites pugnabant, et una pariterque cum equitibus accurrere et refugere confueverant. Hoc fæpius facerent, &c.---Cæfaris autem non amplius tres, aut quatuor milites veterani, fi fe convertiffent, et pila viribus contorta in Numidas infeftos conjeciffent, amplius duorum millium numero ad unum terga vertebant; ac rurfus ad aciem paffim, converfis equis, fe colligebant, atque in fpatio confequebantur, et jacula in Legionarios conjiciebant. Cæsar contra ejufmodi hoftium genera copias fuas, non ut imperator exercitum veteranum, victoremque maximis rebus geftis, fed ut laniffa tirones gladiatores condocefacere: quo pede fefe reciperent ab hofte, &c.-----Mirifice enim hoftium levis armatura anxium exercitum ejus atque follicitum habebat: quia et equites deterrebat prœlium inire, propter equorum interitum; quod eos jaculis interficiebat; et legionarium militem defatigabat, propter velocitatem. Gravis enim armatura miles fimul atque ab his infectatus conftiterat, in eofque impetum fecerat, illi veloci curfu facile periculum vitabant.

" light armed foot, who are wonderfully nimble, always mixing and keeping
" equal pace with the cavalry in charging or retiring, fall afresh on the Ro-
" man foot. Thus they frequently renewed the charge, and still retired
" when he endeavoured to bring them to close engagement. If but two or
" three of his veterans faced about and cast their piles with vigor, two thou-
" sand of the enemy would fly, then returning rally again, making it their
" business to harrass his march, and to press upon his rear, following at some
" distance and throwing their darts at the legions.

" Cæsar, having so subtil an enemy to deal with, instructed his soldiers,
" not like a general who had been victorious in the most arduous exploits, but
" as a ‡ Fencing-Master would instruct his scholars; teaching them with
" what pace to retreat from the enemy, and how to return to the charge ; how
" far to advance, and how far to retire ; and likewise in what place and man-
" ner to cast their piles.   For their light-armed infantry gave him the
" greatest uneasiness, deterring his troopers from meeting them, by killing
" their horses with their javelins, and wearying his legions by their swiftness.
" For whenever his heavy-armed foot faced about, and endeavoured to re-
" turn their charge, they quickly avoided the danger by flight."

But without going back to the ancients, we have seen this maxim adopted
in our days.   Marshal de Saxe finding the French army harrassed by the Hussars and other Austrian light troops, formed also several corps of them of different kinds ; and the king of Prussia in his first war introduced them into his
army, and has augmented and employed them ever since with success.   We
have ourselves made use of them in the two last wars in Europe : but the light
troops wanted in America must be trained upon different principles.   The
enemies we have to deal with, are infinitely more active and dangerous than
the Hussars and Pandours ; or even the Africans abovementioned.   For the
American savages, after their rapid incursions, retreat to their towns, at a
great distance from our settlements, through thickety woods almost impenetra-

G 2   ble

‡ Lanista, in Latin, is an instructor of gladiators, which in English can only be translated a ‘ Fen-
‘ cing-master."

ble to our heavy and unwieldy corps, compofed of foldiers loaded with cloathes, baggage and provifions, who, when fatigued by a long march, muft be a very unequal match to engage the nimble favage in woods, which are his native element.

ANOTHER unavoidable incumbrance in our expeditions, arifes from the provifions and baggage of the army, for which a road muft be opened, and bridges thrown over rivers and fwamps. This creates great labour, retards and weakens the line of march, and keeps the troops tied to a convoy which they cannot lofe fight of, without expofing it to become a prey to a vigilant enemy, continually hovering about to feize every advantage.

AN European, to be a proper judge of this kind of war, muft have lived fometime in the vaft forefts of America; otherwife he will hardly be able to conceive a continuity of woods without end. In fpite of his endeavours, his imagination will betray him into an expectation of open and clear grounds, and he will be apt to calculate his Manoeuvres accordingly, too much upon the principles of war in Europe.

LET us fuppofe a perfon, who is entirely unacquainted with the nature of this fervice, to be put at the head of an expedition in America. We will further fuppofe that he has made the difpofitions ufual in Europe for a march, or to receive an enemy; and that he is then attacked by the favages. He cannot difcover them, tho' from every tree, log or bufh, he receives an inceffant fire, and obferves that few of their fhot are loft. He will not hefitate to charge thofe invifible enemies, but he will charge in vain. For they are as cautious to avoid a clofe engagement, as indefatigable in harraffing his troops; and notwithftanding all his endeavours, he will ftill find himfelf furrounded by a circle of fire, which like an artificial horizon follows him every where.

UNABLE to rid himfelf of an enemy who never ftands his attacks, and flies when preffed, only to return upon him again with equal agility and vigor; he will fee the courage of his heavy troops droop, and their ftrength at laft fail them by repeated and ineffectual efforts.

HE

HE muft therefore think of a retreat, unlefs he can force his way through the enemy. But how is this to be effected? his baggage and provifions are unloaded and fcattered, part of his horfes and drivers killed, others difperfed by fear, and his wounded to be carried by foldiers already fainting under the fatigue of a long action. The enemy encouraged by his diftrefs will not fail to encreafe the diforder, by preffing upon him on every fide, with redoubled fury and favage howlings.

HE will probably form a circle or a fquare, to keep off fo daring an enemy, ready at the leaft opening to fall upon him with the deftructive Tomahawk: but thefe difpofitions, tho' a tolerable fhift for defence, are neither proper for an attack, nor a march thro' the woods-----

THIS is not an imaginary fuppofition, but the true ftate of an engagement with the Indians, experienced by the troops who have fought againft them. Neither is there any thing new or extraordinary in this way of fighting, which feems to have been common to moft * Barbarians.

WHAT is then to be done to extricate our little army from impending deftruction?

THIS is a problem which I do not pretend to refolve. But as every man would, in fimilar circumftances, determine himfelf fome way or other, I will propofe my own fentiments, founded upon fome obfervations which I believe invariable in all engagements with favages.

THE firft, that their general maxim is to furround their enemy.

THE fecond, that they fight fcattered, and never in a compact body.

The third, that they never ftand their ground when attacked, but immediately give way, to return to the charge.

Thefe

---

* Vid. Cæf. comm. lib. V de bello Gallico, et lib. II de bello Civili.

Thefe principles being admitted, it follows------

1ft. That the troops deftined to engage Indians, muft be lightly cloathed, armed, and accoutred.

2d. That having no refiftance to encounter in the attack or defence, they are not to be drawn up in clofe order, which would only expofe them without neceffity to a greater lofs.

AND laftly, that all their evolutions muft be performed with great rapidity; and the men enabled by exercife to purfue the enemy clofely, when put to flight, and not give them time to rally.

THESE remarks will explain the reafons of the alterations propofed in the formation of a corps of troops, for the fervice of the woods. It is not, however, to be expected that this method will remove all obftacles, or that thofe light troops can equal the favages in patience, and activity; but, with difcipline and practice, they may in a great meafure fupply the want of thefe advantages, and by keeping the enemy at a diftance afford great relief and fecurity to the main body.

S E C T I O N II.

GENERAL IDEA OF AN ESTABLISHMENT OF LIGHT TROOPS, FOR THE SERVICE OF THE WOODS.

I fhall only venture a few notions fuggefted by experience upon this fubject, chiefly with a view to recommend it to the confideration of perfons capable of propofing a proper method of forming fuch an eftablifhment: and in order to be better underftood, I will fuppofe a corps of 500 men to be raifed and difciplined for the woods, befides two troops of light horfe, to which a company of artificers might be added. The fitteft men for that fervice would be the natives of America bred upon the frontiers, and inlifted between the age of 15 and 20 years, to be difcharged between 30 and 35.

CLOATHING.

CLOATHING.

THE cloathing of a soldier for the campaign might consist of a short coat of brown cloth, lappelled, and without plaits ; a strong tanned shirt, short trowsers, leggins, mokawsons or shoe packs, a sailors hat, a blanket, a knapsack for provisions, and an oiled * surtout against the rain. To this might be added, in winter quarters or time of peace, three white shirts and stocks, with a flannel waistcoat.

ARMS.

THEIR arms, the best that could be made, should be short fusils and some rifles, with bayonets in the form of a dirk, to serve for a knife ; with powder horns and shot pouches, small hatchets and leathern bottles for water.

EXERCISES.

THE soldiers being raised, cloathed, and formed into companies under proper officers, must, before they are armed, be taught to keep themselves
clean

---

* The following Watch-coat was contrived by an officer, whose name I do not remember. But instead of the oiled linnen to be put under the hat, a cap might perhaps answer better. He writes as follows, viz.

" As the Indian war will require frequent incursions into a wild country, where a man sick or " wounded, is in several respects more detrimental to the service than a man killed, every thing that " may contribute to the health of the men is of moment.

" In this view, I propose a sort of surtout, to preserve men in a great measure both from wet and cold.

" Take a large checked shirt, of about half a crown sterling per yard, for it should be pretty fine ; " cut off the wrist-bands, and continue the opening of the breast down to the bottom ; sew up the sides " from the gussets downwards ; rip out the gathers in the fore parts of the collar as far as the shoulder " straps, and resew it plain to the collar.

" The shirt will then become a sort of watch coat like a bed gown, with very wide sleeves.

" Take a quantity of linseed oil, and boil it gently till one half is diminished, to which put a small " quantity of litharge of gold, and when it is well incorporated with the oil, lay it on with a brush " upon the watch-coat, so that it shall be every where equally wet.

" I suppose the watch coat, hung in a garret, or other covered place, and so suspended by crooked " pins and packthreads in the extremities of the sleeves and edges of the collar, that one part shall " not touch another. In a short time, if the weather is good, it will be dry ; when a second mixture " of the same kind should be laid on with a brush as before. When the second coat of painting is " dry, the grease will not come off and the surtout is an effectual preservative from rain ; it is very " light to carry, and being pretty full on the back, will not only keep the man dry, but also his pack " and ammunition.

" The sleves are left long and wide, to receive the but end of a firelock (secured) and to cover it be- " low the lock. The coat is double breasted to be lapped over, according to which side the rain drives. " A man will be kept dry by one of these surtouts as far as the knees. If, from the vicinity of the " enemy, it is improper to make fires at night, he may place his pack on a stone, and sitting upon it, " change his shoes and leggins, and, if he pleases, wrap his blanket round his legs and feet, then draw- " ing the watchcoat close to his body, it will keep him warm, as no air can pass through it, and, lean- " ing against the trunk of a tree, he may pass a tolerable night, both warm and dry.

" It would be of service to have a small piece of the same oiled linnen to put under the hat or cap " to carry the rain down to the watchcoat or surtout, otherwise whatever wet soaks through the hat " or cap, will run down the neck, and thereby in some measure defeat the design of the watchcoat.

" Perhaps it might be useful to mix some dark or greenish colour with the oil of the second coating, " to make the watchcoat less remarkable in the woods."

clean, and to drefs in a foldier like manner. This will raife in them a becoming fpirit, give them a favourable opinion of their profeffion, and preferve their health. The firft thing they are to learn is to Walk well, afterwards to Run; and in order to excite emulation, fmall premiums might from time to time be given to thofe who diftinguifh themfelves. They muft then run in ranks, with open files, and wheel in that order, at firft flowly, and by degrees increafe their fpeed: this evolution is difficult, but of the utmoft confequence to fall unexpectedly upon the flank of the enemy. They are to difperfe and rally at given fignals; and particular colours fhould be given to each company, for them to rally by; the men muft be ufed to * leap over logs and ditches, and to carry burthens proportioned to their ftrength.

WHEN the young foldiers are perfect in thefe exercifes, they may receive their arms, with which they are to perform the former evolutions in all forts of grounds. They will next be taught to handle their arms with dexterity; and, without lofing time upon trifles, to load and fire very quick, ftanding, kneeling, or lying on the ground. They are to fire at a mark without a reft, and not fuffered to be too long in taking aim. Hunting and fmall premiums will foon make them expert markfmen.

They ought to learn to fwim, pufhing at the fame time their cloathes, arms, and ammunition before them, on a fmall raft; and to make ufe of fnow fhoes. They muft then be fet to work, and be taught to throw up an intrenchment, open a trench, make fafcines, clays and gabions; likewife to fall trees, fquare logs, faw planks, make canoes, carts, ploughs, hand and wheel barrows, fhingles and clap-boards, cafks, batteaus and bridges, and to build log houfes, ovens, &c.

BY example and practice, the moft ingenious among them will foon become tolerable good carpenters, joyners, wheelwrights, coopers, armourers, fmiths,

mafons,

---

* Vegetius gives an account of many fimilar exercifes, which the Romans found neceffary to eftablifh among their military. Miles fylvam cædebat, æftivistemporibus natabat, ad palum dimicabat, faltaoat, currebat. Exempla hujus exercitationis crebra funt apud Livium. Sic ille de Scipione Africano 3. decad. lib VI. " Primo die legiones in armis IV. millium fpatio decurrerunt. " Secundo die arma curare et tergere ante tentoria juffit. Tertio die fudibus inter fe in modum juftæ " pugnæ concurrerent, præpilatisque miffilibus jaculati funt. Quarto die quies data. Quinto " iterum in armis decurfum eft"----Quibus porro modis obviam eatur elephantis. Veget. lib. III. cap. 24.

masons, brickmakers, saddlers, taylors', butchers, bakers, shoemakers, curriers, &c.

L I G H T   H O R S E   and   D O G S.

I said that to compleat this establishment they should have two troops of light horse, supposed of 50 men each, officers included. The men are to perform the same exercises as the foot, and afterwards be taught to ride, and particularly to be very alert at mounting and dismounting with their arms in their hands, to gallop through the woods up and down hills, and leap over logs and ditches.

THE horses ought to be bought up on the frontiers, where they are bred and used to feed in the woods, and are strong and hardy. They are to be thoroughly broke, made to stand fire, to swim over rivers, &c. their saddles and accoutrements very simple strong and light. The number of horses might be reduced to one half, in time of peace, tho' they would be of little expence, as they might be bred and maintained without charge in the military settlement. This corps should be equiped as the foot, having only a short rifle in lieu of a fusil, and a battle ax with a long handle, the only sort of arms they should make use of in the charge.

EVERY light horse man ought to be provided with a Blood-hound, which would be useful to find out the enemies ambushes, and to follow their tracts; they would seize the naked savages, or at least give time to the horse men to come up with them; they would add to the safety of the camp at night by discovering any attempt to surprise it.

A R T I F I C E R S.

THE company of artificers should be composed of the most useful tradesmen, and ought to be maintained at all times for the instruction of the soldiers, the use of the settlement, or the service of the army, during the campaign. It will now be time to draw forth this military colony and remove them to

H   the

the ground laid out for that ufe in the woods, and at a good diftance from the inhabitants, The nature of this fettlement will hereafter be more particularly defcribed.

NECESSITY creating induftry, our young foldiers will foon provide them-felves with the moft ufeful articles, and in a couple of years be able to raife provifions for themfelves.

WHILE the greateft part would be employed in clearing the ground, fencing, ploughing, fowing, planting, building and making utenfils and houfhold furniture, others might hunt with their officers, and remain a fortnight or a month out of the camp, without other provifions than a little flour, and what they could procure by hunting and fifhing: then to be relieved, and the whole trained up in that way.

THE military exercifes muft ftill be kept up and practifed, and great care taken to inculcate and preferve purity of manners, obedience, order and decency among the men, which will be found much eafier in the woods than in the neighbourhood of towns.

IN order to make this military eftablifhment more generally ufeful; I would propofe that the foldiers fhould only receive a very fmall part of their pay; leaving the remainder in the military cheft.

THEIR accounts fhould be fettled every year, and when their fervices fhould intitle them to their difcharge, I could wifh that each of them had 200 acres of land given him, in a diftrict appropriated for that purpofe ; and receiving then the whole ballance of pay due to them, they would be enabled to compleat their fettlement. This inftitution appears not only practicable, but eafy, if attended to with patience, affiduity and firmnefs. The plan I would propofe is as follows.

METHOD

METHOD of forming such SETTLEMENTS upon the FRON-
TIERS, as might support themselves during an INDIAN-WAR.

LET us suppose a settlement to be form'd for one hundred families, composed of five persons each, upon an average.

LAY out upon a river, or creek, if it can be found conveniently, a SQUARE
of one thousand seven hundred and sixty yards, or a mile for each side.

THAT Square will contain - - - - - - - - - - - - 640 acres
Allowing for streets and publick uses   - - - - - - 40 ⎞
To half an acre for every house   -   -   -   - 50 ⎬ 640 acres
To 100 lotts at five and half acres   -   -   - - 550 ⎠

THE four sides of the square measure 7040 yards, which gives to each house
about 70 yards front to stockade, and the ground allowed for building will be
210 feet front, and about 100 feet deep.

AN acre of ground will produce at least 30 bushels of Indian corn. Therefore, two acres are sufficient to supply five persons, at the rate of twelve
bushels each person. Two other acres will be a pasture for cowes and sheep,
another acre for hay, to be sown with red clover. The remaining half acre
may be laid out for a garden.

ROUND the town are the commons, of three miles square, containing, ex-
clusive of the lots abovementioned, 5120 acres. On three sides of the town,
five other Squares will be laid out of three square miles, containing 5760
acres each, one of which is reserved for wood for the use of the Settlement;
the other four to be divided into 25 out-lotts or plantations, of about 230
acres each, so that in the four Squares, there will be one hundred such plantations, for the 100 families.

ANOTHER township may be laid out joining this, upon the same plan, and
as many more as you please upon the same line, without loosing any ground.

H 2   THE

The following is a rough sketch of the whole.

Township A.   Township B.   Township C.   Township D.

I	I	2	2	3	3	4	4
5760 acres wood for the Town A	Commons A Commons	Commons B Commons	Wood for the Town B	Wood for the Town C	Commons C Commons	Commons D Commons	Wood for the Town D
25 lotts of 230 acres 1	1	2	2	3	3	4	4

Thus the town, A, has its commons, its woodland, and its 4 squares marked No. 1. each containing 25 plantations of 230 acres, as proposed above. In like manner, the other towns, B, C, D, have their appurtenances respectively marked.

Let us now suppose this plan accomplished, and such corps as these fully settled, trained and disciplined, in the manner abovementioned; I would ask whether any officer, entrusted with an expedition against the savages, would not chuse to have them in his army? I may safely answer for all those who have been employed in that service, that they would prefer them to double the number of the best European troops. And when they had served the time limited, namely from their 15th to their 35th year, what vast satisfaction would it be to pay over to them their share of savings from the publick chest; and, as a reward of their faithful toils, to vest them and their heirs with their several plantations, which they would now be enabled to cultivate as their own? This prospect would engage many people to enter their sons, in such corps; and those veterans, when thus discharged, would not only be the means of forming and animating others by their example, but in case of a war would

still

ftill bravely maintain the property they had fo honorably acquired, and be the greateft fecurity of the frontier where they are fettled.

PREPARATIONS FOR AN EXPEDITION IN THE WOODS AGAINST SAVAGES.

IT is not practicable to employ large bodies of troops againft Indians ; the convoys neceffary for their fupport would be too cumberfome, and could neither be moved with eafe, nor protected.   It would be better to fit out feveral fmall expeditions, than one too unwieldy : I will therefore fuppofe that a corps intended to act offenfively fhall not exceed the following proportions.

Two regiments of foot - - - - - - - - - - 900
One battalion of hunters - - - - - - - - - 500
Two troops of light horfe - - - - - - - - - 100
One company of artificers - - - - - - - - 20
Drivers and neceffary followers - - - - - - 280

In all   1800

THE firft article to provide is the provifions, and next the carriages.

THE daily ration of a foldier in the woods fhould confift of one pound and a half of meat (which requires no carriage) and one pound of flour, with a gill of falt per week.

UPON that allowance 1800 men will require for fix months or 182 days - - - - - } 327,600 lb. Flour.

ALLOWING one fourth for accident - - - 81,900
For fix months   409,500 lb. Flour.

Meat for the fame time with a fourth part more for accidents, or 2048 beeves at 300 lb. each } 614,400 lb. Meat.

Salt for 26 weeks - - - - - - - 182 Bufhells.

THE above quantity would ferve the whole campaign, but one half would be fufficient to penetrate from the laft depofite into the heart of the enemy's country : therefore we fhall compute the carriages for this laft quantity only.

EVERY horfe carries about 150 lb. neat weight, therefore, to carry flour for three months or 204,750 lb. will require 1365 horfes.

HORSES

HORSES for flour brought forward   -   -   Ɩ   1365
For 91 bushels of salt   -   -   -   -   -   46
Ammunition   -   -   -   -   -   50
Tents   -   -   -   -   -   -   -   50
Tools   -   -   -   -   -   -   -   50
Hospital   -   -   -   -   -   -   20
Officers baggage and staff   -   -   -   -   150

                                                    1731

To reduce this exhorbitant number of horses, and the great expence attending it, I would propose, for such parts of the country as would admit of it, to make use of carts, drawn each by four oxen, and carrying about 1300 lb. or six barrels of flour.   The above quantity of 204,750 lb. will then be carried by 160 carts drawn by   -   -   -   -   -   - 640 oxen
Spare oxen with the army   -   -   -   384
                    The number of oxen wanted   -   1024

THIS method would not be as expeditious as the carriage by horses, and would require more time and attention in cutting the road, and bridging the swampy places &c ; but, on the other hand, what an expence would be saved ! and by killing the oxen in proportion as the flour is used, and abandoning the carts, the convoy is daily reduced, and t'e grass near the encampment will not be so soon consumed, which is not the case with horses, which must equally be fed though unloaded.   This is an object of consequence, particularly near the end of the campaign, when the scarcity of fodder obliges to move the camps every day, and to place them in low and disadvantageous grounds.

I WOULD therefore incline for the use of carts, and they could be made before hand by the hunters and their artificers.

THE oxen should be bought in the provinces where the farmers make use of them in their works. One or two soldiers would drive the cart and take charge of the four oxen.

                                                    THERE

THERE are few rivers in North-America deep in summer, and which these carts with high and broad wheels, could not ford ; but if the contrary should happen, the carts, provisions and baggage, may be rafted over, or a bridge built. In a country full of timber, and with troops accustomed to work, no river will stop an army for a long time.

By the above method, 3 or 400 horses would be sufficient to carry the baggage ammunition, tents, tools &c.

E X P L A N A T I O N OF THE FOUR PLANS, † PLATE II.
Representing the different positions of our army in the woods.

E N C A M P M· E N T.

THE camp (Fig. 1) forms a parralellogram, of one thousand by six hundred feet. Eight hundred men of the regular troops (1) encamp on the four sides, which gives twenty-four feet to each tent, containing six men. The light-horse (3) encamp within the parrallelogram. The reserve (7) in the center.

THE provisions, ammunition, tools and stores (8) and the cattle (9) are placed between the two troops of light-horse and the reserve. The hunters (2) encamp on the outside diagonally at the four angles, being covered by redoubts (5) formed with kegs and bags of flour or fascines. Besides these four redoubts, another is placed to the front, one to the rear, and two before each of the long faces of the camp, making in all ten advanced guards of 22 men each, and 7 centries, covered if possible by breast works of fascines or provisions. Before the army lay down their arms, the ground is to be reconnoitred, and the guards posted, who will immediately open a communication from one to the other, to relieve the centries, and facilitate the passage of rounds.

THE centries upon the ammunition, provisions, head quarters, and all others in the inside of the camp are furnished from the reserve. The officers, except the staff and commanders of corps, encamp on the line with their men.

THE

† See this Plate before Pag. 7.

THE fires are made between the guards and camp, and put out in cafe of an attack in the night.

LINE of MARCH, Plate II. Fig. II.

PART of the hunters (2) in three divifions detaching fmall parties (5, 6) to their front and to their right and left, to fearch the woods and difcover the enemy.

THE artificers and ax-men (4) to cut a road for the convoy, and two paths on the right and left for the troops.

ONE hundred and fifty of the regular troops (1) in two files, who are to form the front of the fquare ; thefe march in the center road.

Two hundred and fifty regulars (1) in one file by the right hand path ; and 250 (1) by the left hand path, are to form the long faces.

THESE are followed by 150 regulars (1) in two files, who are to form the rear of the fquare.

THE referve (7) compos'd of 100 regulars in two files.

THE reft of the hunters (2) in two files.

THE light horfe (3.)

THE rear guard (5) compos'd of hunters, follows the convoy at fome diftance and clofes the march. The fcouting parties (6) who flank the line of march, are taken from the hunters and light horfe, and pofted as in plan (Fig. 2) fome orderly light horfe men, attend the General and field officers who command the grand divifions, to carry their orders. Two guards of light horfe take charge of the cattle (9.)

THE convoy (8) proceeds in the following order

THE tools and ammunition following the front column.

THE baggage.

THE cattle.   THE

THE provifions.

THE whole divided into Brigades, and the horfes two a breaft.

DEFILES.

IN cafe of a defile, the whole halt until the ground is reconnoitred, and the hunters have taken poffeffion of the heights. The center column then enters in to the defile, followed by the right-face ; after them the convoy, then the left and rear face, with the referve, the light horfe, and the rear guard.

THE whole to form again as foon as the ground permits.

DISPOSITION TO RECEIVE THE ENEMY, Fig. (3)

THE whole halt to form the fquare or parrallelogram, which is done thus. The two firft men of the center column ftand faft at two yards diftance. The two men following them, ftep forward and poft themfelves at two yards on the right and left. The others come to the front in the fame manner, till the two files have form'd a rank, which is the front of the fquare.

THE rear face is formed by the two file-leaders turning to the center road, where having placed themfelves at two yards diftance, they face outwards, and are followed by their files, each man pofting himfelf on their right or left, and facing towards the enemy the moment he comes to his poft.

As foon as the front and rear are extended and formed, the two long faces, who have in the mean time faced outwards, join now the extremities of the two fronts and clofe the fquare. †

TO REDUCE THE SQUARE.

THE right and left of the front, face to the center, where the two center men ftand faft. Upon the word " march" thefe ftep forward and are replaced by the two next, who follow them, and fo on; by which means, that front becomes again a column. The rear goes to the

I

right

† Thefe evolutions muft be performed with celerity.

right about, and each of the two center men leads again to the side paths followed by the rest.

While the troops form, the light horse and each division of the convoy take the ground assigned to them within the square, as if they were to encamp; and the horses being unloaded, two parrallel lines will be formed, with the bags and kegs of provisions, to cover the wounded and the men unfit for action. The hunters take post on the most advantageous ground on the out side, and skirmish with the enemy, till the square is form'd; when, upon receiving their orders, they retire within the square, where they take their post as in Fig. (3)

The small parties of rangers (5) who have flanked the line of march, remain on the outside, to keep off the enemy and observe their motions.

When the firing begins the troops will have orders to fall on their knees, to be less exposed till its thought proper to attack.

The four faces, form'd by the regular troops, are divided into platoons *chequer'd.* One half, composed of the best and most active soldiers, is called the first Firing, and the other half the second Firing.

The eight platoons at the angles are of the second Firing, in order to preserve the form of the square during the attack.

It is evident that, by this disposition, the convoy is well cover'd, and the light troops, destined for the charge, remain concealed; and as all unexpected events during an engagement are apt to strike terror, and create confusion, among the enemy, it is natural to expect that the savages will be greatly disconcerted at the sudden and unforeseen eruption, that will soon pour upon them from the inside of the square; and that, being vigorously attacked in front and flank at the same time, they will neither be able to resist, nor, when once broke, have time to rally, so as to make another stand. This may be effected in the following manner.

GENERAL

GENERAL ATTACK, Fig. IV.

THE Regulars (1) ftand faft.

THE hunters (2) fally out, in four columns, through the intervals of the front and rear of the fquare, followed by the light horfe (3) with their blood-hounds.   The intervals of the two columns who attack in the front, and of thofe who attack in the rear, will be clofed by the little parties of rangers (5) pofted at the angles of the fquare, each attack forming in that manner, three fides of a parrallelogram. In that order they run to the enemy (X) and having forced their way through their circle, fall upon their flanks; by wheeling to their right and left, and charging with impetuofity. The moment they take the enemy in flank, the Firft Firing of the regular troops march out brifkly and attack the enemy in front.   The platoons detached in that manner from the two fhort faces, proceed only about one hundred yards to their front, where they halt to cover the fquare, while the reft of the troops who have attacked purfue the enemy, till they are totally difperfed, not giving them time to recover themfelves.

THE fick and wounded, unable to march or ride, are tranfported in litters made of flour bags, through which two long poles are paffed, and kept afunder by two fticks, tied acrofs beyond the head and feet to ftretch the bag.   Each litter is carried by two horfes———

THESE remarks might have been extended to many other cafes that may occur in the courfe of a campaign or of an engagement, but it is hoped this fketch will be fufficient to evince the neceffity of fome alteration in our ordinary method of proceeding in an Indian war.

APPENDIX I.

CONSTRUCTION of FORTS

AGAINST

INDIANS.

A S we have not to guard here againſt cannon, the ſyſtem of European fortifications may be laid aſide, as expenſive, and not anſwering the purpoſe. Forts againſt Indians, being commonly remote from our ſettlements, require a great deal of room to lodge a ſufficient quantity of ſtores and proviſions, and at the ſame time ought to be defenſible with one half of their compleat garriſons, in caſe of detachments or convoys.

I am therefore of opinion that a ſquare or pentagon, with a block-houſe of brick or ſtone * at every angle, joined by a wall flanked by the block-houſes, would be the beſt defence againſt ſuch enemies. A ditch from ſeven to eight feet deep might be added, with loop holes in the cellars of the block-houſes ſix feet from the ground, to defend the ditch.

ALONG the inſide of the curtains the traders might build houſes and ſtores, covered as well as the block-houſes with tiles, or ſlate, to guard againſt fire arrows. There will remain a ſpacious area for free air and uſe, in which as well as in the ditch, gardens might be made and wells dug.

THE

* Experience has demonſtrated that fortifications made of wood decay very ſoon, and are on that account of conſiderable expence.

The powder magazines might be placed in the center of the area, keeping only a small quantity of cartridges in each block-house for present use.

The garrisons of such forts would be free from surprises, even if they had no centries, for nothing can get at them, while the doors are well bolted and barred.

Some Reasons for keeping Possession of our large Forts in the Indian Country.

As these forts have been one of the causes of the last war and are a great eye-fore to the savages, they have bent their chief efforts against them ; and therefore, while thus employed, they have been less able to distress our settlements. Our forts keep the Indian towns at a great distance from us. Fort-Pitt has effectually driven them beyond the Ohio, and made them remove their settlements at least 60 miles further westward. Was it not for these forts, they would settle close on our borders, and in time of war infest us every day in such numbers as would over-power the thin inhabitants scattered on our extensive frontier. The farmer unable to sow or reap would soon fall back on our chief towns, or quit the country for want of bread. In either case, what would be the fate of the large towns burthened with the whole country, and depriv'd of subsistance and of the materials of trade and export ?

The destruction of these forts being, in time of war, the chief aim of the savages, they gather about them to distress the garrisons, and to attack the convoys ; thereby giving us an opportunity to fight them in a body, and to strike a heavy blow, which otherwise they would never put in our power, as their advantage lies in surprizes, which are best effected by small numbers. Experience has convinced them that it is not in their power to break those shackles, and therefore it is not probable that they will renew the attempt ; and our posts will continue a check upon them, and save the difficulty and expence of taking post again in their country. Our forts are likewise the proper places for trade, which being closely inspected, it will be easy for us to limit their

supplies

supplies, to such commodities as they cannot turn against us, and to put a speedy stop to all just causes of complaints, by giving immediate redress.

A few forts, with strong garrisons, I should judge to be of more service than a greater number weakly guarded. In the last war we lost all our small posts : but our more considerable ones, Detroit and Fort-Pitt, resisted all the efforts of the savages, by the strength of their garrisons.

A P P E N D I X II.

THE following Paper was written by an Officer well acquainted with the places he describes; and is thought worthy of a place here, as every thing is material which can encrease our knowlege of the vast countries ceded to us and of the various nations that inhabit them.

Account of the French Forts ceded to Great Britain in Louisiana.

THE settlement of the Illinois being in 40 degrees of latitude, is 500 leagues from New-Orleans by water and 350 by land.

THE most proper time of the year for going there, is the begining of February. The waters of the Missisippi are then high, and the country being overflowed, there is less to fear from the savages, who are hunting in that season.

THE encampments should be on the left of the river, as the enemies are on the right, and cannot have a sufficient number of crafts to cross if their party is large.

THEY generally attack at day-break, or at the time of embarking.

THE inhabitants of the Illinois might bring provisions half way, if they were allowed good pay.

THE

The Delawares and Shawanese lie near Fort Du Quesne, * which is about 500 leagues from the Ilinois. The Wiandots and Ottawas, (who are at the Detroit) are about 250 leagues from the Ilinois by land. And the Miamis about 200 by land.

Nevertheless as intelligence is carried very faft by the Savages, and as all the nations with whom we are at war, can come by the Ohio, § we muft be vigilant to prevent a furprife.

The mouth of the Ohio, in the Miffifippi, is 35 leagues from the Illinois.

Thirteen leagues from the Miffifippi on the left, or eaft fide of the Ohio, is Fort Maffiac, or Affumption, built in 1757, a little below the mouth of the river ‡ Cherokee. It is only a ftockade, with four baftions and eight pieces of cannon. It may contain 100 men. In four days one may go by land, from this fort to the Ilinois.

It is of confequence for the Englifh to preferve it, as it fecures the communication between the Ilinois and Fort-Pitt.

Fort Vincennes, which is the laft poft belonging to Louifiana, is upon the river † Ouabache, 60 leagues from its conflux with the Ohio. It is a fmall ftockade fort, in which there may be about 20 foldiers. There are alfo a few inhabitants. The foil is extremely fertile, and produces plenty of corn and tobacco.

The diftance from this fort to the Ilinois, is 155 leagues by water. And it may be travelled by land in fix days.

The nation of favages living at this poft is called Pianquicha. It can furnish 60 warriors. Altho'

* So the French formerly called what is now Fort Pitt.
§ Part of the navigation of the Ohio, from Fort-Pitt is defcribed as follows, viz.
That the difficult part of the river is from Fort-Pitt about 50 or 60 miles downwards. There are 52 iflands between Fort-Pitt and the lower Shawanefe Town on Scioto ; and none of them difficult to pafs in the night, but one at the mouth of Mufkingham, occafioned by a number of trees lying in the channel. From the lower Shawanefe Town to the falls, there are but 8 or 9 iflands. At the falls, the river is very broad, with only one paffage on the eaft fide, in which there is water enough at all feafons of the year to pafs without difficulty. Below the falls, the navigation is every way clear, down to the Miffifippi.
‡ River Cherokee falls into the Ohio about 800 miles below Fort-Pitt. This river is in general wide and fhoal up to the fouth mountain, paffable only with bark canoes, after which it grows very fmall.
† Ouabache or Wabafh empties itfelf into the Ohio about 60 miles above the Cherokee river, on the oppofite or weft fide.

ALTHO' we do not occupy Fort Vincennes at prefent, yet it would be of the utmoft confequence for us to fettle it, as there is a communication from it with Canada, by going up the Ouabache.

FROM this poft to the Ouachtanons is 60 leagues, and from thence to the Miamis (ftill going up the Oubache) is 60 leagues further; then there is a portage of fix leagues to the river Miamis, and you go down that river 24 leagues to Lake Erie.

MR. DAUBRY went by that rout in 1759 from the Ilinois to * Venango, with above 400 men, and two hundred thoufand weight of flour.

THIRTY-five leagues from the mouth of the Ohio, in going up the Miffi-fippi, on the right, is the river Kafkafquias. Two leagues up this river, on the left, is the fettlement of the Kafkafquias, which is the moft confiderable of the Ilinois.

THERE is a fort built upon the height on the other fide of the river, over againft Kafkafquias; which, as the river is narrow, commands and pro-tects the town.

I DON'T know how many guns there may be, nor how many men it may contain. There may be about 400 inhabitants.

THE Ilinois Indians, called Kafkafquias, are fettled half a league from the town; and are able to turn out 100 warriors. They are very lazy and great drunkards.

K   THE

* By the above paper the rout is given up the Miffifippi, part of the Ohio, and up the Ouabache to Fort Vincennes, and likewife to the Ilinois. Again from Vincennes and the Ouachtanons by water, to the Miamis portage; then by water down that river by the eafterly rout into Lake Erie, proceeding as far as Prefqu' Ifle, then by the 15 m. portage into Buffalo or Beef river, lately called French creek, then down the fame to Venango on the Ohio. In order, therefore, to carry this rout ftill further, we fhall continue it from Venango to the mouth of Juniata in Sufquehannah, which brings it within the fettled parts of Pennfylvania, viz.
From Venango to Licking creek, 10 miles. To Toby's creek, 13. To a fmall creek, 1. To the parting of the road, 5. To a large run, 3. To Leycaumeyhoning, 9. To Pine creek, 7. To Chuckcaughting, 8. To Weeling creek, 4. To the crofling of ditto, 4. To a miry fwamp, 8. To the head of Sufquehanna, 10. To Meytauning creek, 18. To Clear Field creek, 6. To the top of Allegheny, 1. To the other fide ditto, 6. To Beaver dams 5. To Franks town, 5. To tne Cannoe place, 6. To the mouth of Juniatta, 110. Total 239 miles.

Six Leagues from Kaſkaſquias, on the bank of the Miſſiſippi, is Fort Chartres, built of ſtone, and can contain 300 ſoldiers. There may be 20 cannon at moſt, and about 100 inhabitants round Chartres.

The Ilinois Indians at that place, who are called Metchis, can furniſh 40 warriors.

Between the Kaſkaſquias, and Fort Chartres, is a ſmall village, called *La prairie du Rocher* (the Rock Meadow) containing about 50 white inhabitants; but there is neither fort nor ſavages.

Near Fort Chartres is a little village, in which is about a ſcore of inhabitants. Here are neither ſavages nor fort.

Fifteen leagues from Fort Chartres, going up the Miſſiſipi is the village of the Caſquiars. There is a ſmall ſtockade fort; I don't know if there is any cannon. There may be about 100 inhabitants.

The Ilinois Indians living near this village are called Caſquiars and can turn out 60 warriors.

I compute that there are about 300 Negroes at the Ilinois.

The country of the Ilinois is fertile, producing good wheat and corn. All kinds of European fruits ſucceed there ſurprizingly well, and they have wild grapes with which they make tolerable wine. Their beer is pretty good.

There are mines of lead, and ſome ſalt. They make ſugar of Maple, and there are ſtone quaries.

A P P E N D I X III.

NUMBER of INDIAN TOWNS, fituated on and near the Ohio River, and its branches, with their diftances from Fort-Pitt, and the diftances of the principal branches from each other at their conflux with the Ohio.

	Diſtance from one another.	Diſtance from Fort Pitt.
FIRST ROUT about N. N. W.	Miles	Miles
From FORT PITT to Kuſhkuſkies Town on Big Beaver Creek		45
up the eaſt branch of Beaver-Creek to Shaningo	15	60
up ditto to Pematuning	12	72
to Mohoning on the Weſt branch of Beaver-Creek.	32	104
up the branch to Salt Lick	10	114
to Cayahoga River	32	146
to Ottawas town on Cayahoga	10	156
SECOND ROUT W. N. W.		
From FORT PITT to the mouth of Big Beaver-Creek		25
to Tuſcarawas	91	116
to Mohickon John's Town	50	166
to Junundat or Wyandot town	46	212
to Fort Sanduſky	4	216
to Junqueindundeh	24	240
THIRD ROUT about W. S. W.		
From FORT PITT to the Forks of the Muſkingham		128
to Bullet's Town on Muſkingham	6	134
to Wakautamike	10	144
to King Beaver's Town on the heads of Hochocking	27	171
to the lower Shawaneſe Town on Sioto river	40	211
to the Salt Lick town on the heads of Sioto	25	236
to the Miamis fort	190	426

FOURTH

	Diftance from one another. Miles	Diftance from FortPitt. Miles
FOURTH ROUT down the Ohio; general courfe about S. W		
By water from FORT PITT to the mouth of Big Beaver Creek		27
to the mouth of Little Beaver Creek	12	39
to the mouth of Yellow Creek	10	49
to the two Creeks	18	67
to Weeling	6	73
to Pipe Hill	12	85
to the long Reach	30	115
to the foot of the Reach	18	133
to the Mouth of Mufkingam river	30	163
to the little Canhawa river	12	175
to the mouth of Hockhocking river	13	188
to the mouth of Letort's creek	40	228
to Kifkeminetas	33	261
to the mouth of big Canhawa or new river	8	269
to the mouth of big Sandy creek	40	309
to the mouth of Sioto River	40	349
to the mouth of big Salt Lick River	30	379
to the Ifland	20	399
to the mouth of little Mineamie or § Miammee	55	454
to big Miammee or Rocky river [river	30	484
to the † Big Bones	20	504
to Kentucky River	55	559
to the Falls of the Ohio	50	609
to the Wabafh, or Ouabache	131	740
to Cherokee River	60	800
to the Miffifippi	40	840
to the Sea down the Miffifippi about	930	1730

N. B. THE places mentioned in the three firft Routs are delineated in the foregoing map, by an officer who has an actual knowledge of moft of them, and has long ferved againft the Indians. The fourth rout down the Ohio was given by an Indian trader, who has often paffed from Fort-Pitt to the Falls; and the diftances he gives of the mouths of the feveral rivers that fall into the Ohio may be pretty certainly depended on. Our maps hitherto publifhed are very erroneous in placing fome of thofe rivers.

§ Thefe rivers called Little and Great Mineamie or Miammee fall into the Ohio between Sioto and the Ouabache, and are different from the Miamis river, which runs into the weft end of lake Erie, below the Miamis fort.
† So called from Elephant's bones faid to be found there.

APPENDIX IV.

N A M E S of different INDIAN NATIONS in NORTH-AMERICA, with the NUMBERS of their FIGHTING MEN; referred to in the note page 37.

THE following lift was drawn up by a French trader, a perfon of confiderable note who has refided many years among the Indians, and ftill continues at Detroit, having taken the oaths of allegiance to the King of Great Britain. His account may be depended on, fo far as matters of this kind can be brought near the truth; a great part of it being delivered from his own perfonal knowlege.

		Warriors
Conawaghrunas, near the falls of St. Louis		200
Abenaquis ⎫		350
Michmacs ⎪		700
* Amaliftes ⎬ St. Lawrence Indians		550
* Chaias ⎭		130
Nipiffins ⎫ living towards the heads of the		400
Algonquins ⎬ Ottawa river		300
Les Tetes de Boule, or Round Heads, near the above		2500
Six Nations, on the frontiers of New-York, &c.		1550
Wiandots, near lake Erie		300
Chipwas ⎫ near the Lakes Superior		5 00
Ottawas ⎬ and Michigan		900
Meffefagues, ⎬ or River Indians, being wandering tribes, on the lakes Huron and Superior		2000
Powtewatamis, near St. Jofeph's and Detroit		350
Les Puans		700
Fo le avoine, or ⎫ near Puans bay Wild-Oat Indians ⎬		350
* Mechecouakis ⎫		250
Sakis ⎬ South of Puans bay		400
Mafcoutens ⎭		500
Ouifconfins, on a river of that name, falling into Miffifippi on the eaft-fide		550

Chriftinaux

Chriftinaux   } far north, near the lakes of the - - - 3000
Affinaboes,   or Affinipouals }   fame name   -   -   -   1500
* Blancs ‡ Barbus,   or White Indians with Beards   -   -   1500
Sioux, of the meadows }   towards the heads   -   -   -   2500
Sioux, of the woods   }   of Miffifippi   -   -   -   1800
Miffouri, on the river of that name   -   -   -   -   3000
* Grandes Eaux   -   -   -   -   1000
Ofages   }   -   -   - -   600
Canfes   } -   -   -   1600
Panis blancs, or white Panis   } fouth of Miffouri   --   2000
Panis piques, freckled or prick Panis }   -   1700
Padoucas   } -   -   -   500
Ajoues, north of the fame   -   -   -   -   1100
Arkanfes,   on the river that bears their name, falling into Miffifippi
               on the weft fide   2000
Alibamous, on the river of their name -   -   -   600
Caouitas, eaft of the former   -   -   -   --   700
* Ouanakina   } Unknown, unlefs the author has put them 300
* Chiakaneffou   }   for tribes of the Creeks   350
* Machecous   }   800
* Souikilas   } -   -   -   -   200
Miamis, upon the river of that name, falling into Lake Erie - - - 350
Delawares (les Loups) on the Ohio   -   -   -   -   600
Shawanefe on Sioto   -   -   -   -   -   500
Kikapous   } -   -   -   -   300
Ouachtenons } on the Ouabache   -   -   -   -   400
Pianquichas }   -   -   -   -   -   250
Kafkafquias, or Ilinois in general, on the Ilinois river   -   -   600
* Pianria   -   -   -   -   -   800
Catawbas, on the Frontiers of North-Carolina   -   -   150
Cherokees, behind South-Carolina   -   -   -   2500
Chickafaws } -   -   -   -   -   750
Natchez   } Mobile and Miffifippi -   -   -   150
Chactaws }   -   -   -   -   4500

                                       56,580

THE above lift confifts chiefly of fuch Indians as the French were connected with in Canada and Louifiana. Wherever we knew the names by which the different nations are diftinguifhed by the Englifh, we have inferted them. But the Orthography is yet very unfettled, and the feveral nations marked with an * Afterifm are unknown to us, and therefore they are left as they ftand in the original lift.

                                              So

‡ They live to the northweft and the French when they firft faw them took them for Spaniards.

So large a number of fighting men may ftartle us at firft fight; but the account feems no where exaggerated, excepting only that the Catawba nation is now almoft extinct. In fome nations which we are acquainted with, the account falls even fhort of their numbers; and fome others do not appear to be mentioned at all, or at leaft not by any name known to us.

Such for inftance are the Lower Creeks, of whom we have a lift according to their towns. In this lift their warriors or gunfmen are 1180, and their inhabitants about 6000. Thus a comparative judgment may be formed of the nations above-mentioned; the number of whofe inhabitants will (in this proportion to their warriors, viz. 5 to 1) be about 283,000.

The number of Indian nations are, however, much fewer than are laid down in the maps. For, in the delineation of thofe remote countries, it has been too often cuftomary with geographers, where ever they could collect names to put them for nations, and affign them a place in their maps, tho' perhaps only towns of fome other nations named at the fame time. There are alfo great changes in the ftate of thefe nations, in the courfe of years. Some are almoft totally deftroyed, and others frequently fo thinned and reduced that they defire adoption into fome more powerful nation, and, being blended with them, lofe their original name.

The END.

ERRATA

Page 17. line 13. *read* impaffable, P. 21. l. 8. from bottom, after word "Delawares" put a full ftop. P. 40. l. 1. *r.* confifts. P. 51. l. laft, *r.* lofing. P. 58. l. 13. for "its" *r.* it is. P. 64. l. 9. *r.* leave out the words, "or the Eaft fide."